Out of The Shadows

Life on the Other Side of the Rainbow

Steven Stehle

STEVEN STEHLE

Copyright © 2021 Steven Stehle

ISBN: 978-1-946106-64-3

All rights reserved. No part of this book may be reproduced or transmitted in any form or by any means, electronic or mechanical, including photocopying, recording, or by an information storage and retrieval system – except by a reviewer who may quote brief passages in a review to be printed in a magazine or newspaper – without permission in writing from the publisher.

Scriptures marked AMP are taken from the AMPLIFIED BIBLE (AMP): Scripture taken from the AMPLIFIED® BIBLE, Copyright © 1954, 1958, 1962, 1964, 1965, 1987 by the Lockman Foundation. Used by Permission. (www.Lockman.org)

Scriptures marked NAS are taken from the NEW AMERICAN STANDARD (NAS): Scripture taken from the NEW AMERICAN STANDARD BIBLE®, copyright© 1960, 1962, 1963, 1968, 1971, 1972, 1973, 1975, 1977, 1995 by The Lockman Foundation. Used by permission.

Scriptures marked NIV are taken from the NEW INTERNATIONAL VERSION (NIV): Scripture taken from THE HOLY BIBLE, NEW INTERNATIONAL VERSION ®. Copyright© 1973, 1978, 1984, 2011 by Biblica, Inc.™. Used by permission of Zondervan.

Scriptures marked KJV are taken from the KING JAMES VERSION (KJV): KING JAMES VERSION, public domain.

Scriptures marked NLT are taken from the HOLY BIBLE, NEW LIVING TRANSLATION (NLT): Scriptures taken from the HOLY BIBLE, NEW LIVING TRANSLATION, Copyright© 1996, 2004, 2007 by Tyndale House Foundation. Used by permission of Tyndale House Publishers, Inc., Carol Stream, Illinois 60188. All rights reserved. Used by permission.

Glorified Publishing
P.O. Box 8004
The Woodlands TX 77387
www.GlorifiedPublishing.com

Printed in the U.S.A.

DEDICATION

In Memory of Jaret and as a Testament to Jason and Jade.
I love you all more than words can express.

STEVEN STEHLE

CONTENTS

	Foreword	vii
	Acknowledgments	ix
	Introduction	xiii
1	Friendless	1
2	Lessons from a Bad Education	9
3	Roots	19
4	The First Time I Came Out of the Closet	33
5	Boom! I'm Straight	43
6	Rocky Roads and Shifty Sand	47
7	Another Lost Battle	57
8	Starting Over	65
9	Birds of a Feather	71

10	The Night the Lights Went Out in Georgia	83
11	The Beach is Not My Home	89
12	And Then There Were Two	95
13	No Longer Negative	113
14	Rehab #1	121
15	Second Chances	129
16	The Valley of Death	147
17	The First Time I Died	161
18	The Road Back Home	179
19	Awakening	203
	Final Thoughts	209
	About The Author	211

FOREWORD

Each one of us has a story. Some are surprisingly simple and predictable, while others are more intricate and complex; but, in the end, they all are unique to us and solely ours to tell. As followers of Christ our stories are part of an even greater narrative because God has allowed us to be a part of His story as well: the story of love and redemption.

Steve Stehle's story is unique and yet universal. A young boy heard the gospel of Jesus, and he was transformed by the love of a Savior. As he grew older, he confronted issues that brought confusion, heartache, and brokenness. Lifestyle choices were made that would seemingly change the course of his life forever. Everything that he had known and loved was taken away.

Our own stories deal with challenges which have different names, but they are all diversions, detours, and distractions, keeping us away from the true identity that God has destined for us. We can feel like there is no way out; no hope for change; no reprieve from the paths we have surged. That could have been the ending of Steve's story, except that God had a different one in mind.

We have known Steve for over thirty years. He is the oldest son of our dear friends, Lanell and Murry Stehle. Steve's parents have been an integral part of his story, not just for their strong foundation in his early years, but also for their unconditional love and constant prayer when he was making choices that violated their own beliefs and standards. As their friends, we, too, began to pray that Steve would see the reality of who he really was; not an identity through a lifestyle, but an identity as a son of the Lord Most High, who loved him and had given His life for him. The love of God, be it to Steve directly, or through the lives of God's people, was the Hope of Steve's redemption and restoration.

It has been said that the gospel is the story of history and YOUR story, interpreted by Love. Here is the gospel of Jesus in the life of Steve Stehle, interpreted by the Author of the most beautiful love story of both heaven and earth.

Jamie and Conrad Appleton
October 1, 2021

ACKNOWLEDGMENTS

I want to thank my family and my parents Murry and Lanell Stehle for all your love and support throughout my life. Your steadfast love for me and your confidence that God had a plan for my life, and the fact that you continued to hold me before Him in prayer, has been the lifeline that kept me safe my entire life. I am blessed to have a sister, Stacie Wommack, who loves me with a faithfulness that is unwavering, will fight for me and never backs down.

I have been blessed in this life to have the love of so many family members. I am most grateful for my great grandmother, "Granny Green", who spent her life in physical pain, but dedicated it to praying for her children, grandchildren, great-grandchildren, and great-great-grandchildren, holding us before the Lord. She never was seen without a smile, no matter how difficult her life had become.

For the love of Christian Warriors like Jim and Tommie Gotcher, Jack and Clair Johnson, Conrad and Jamie Appleton and the friends that stood beside me in my darkest days of addiction, Lance Brock, Corey Fauble, David Harris, Allen Smith, Tony Ward, Jim Fields, Joanie Holt, Anne Bates, Monty Montgomery, Darlene Harris, Stephanie Masterson, Judy and Bill Jackson and Reece, Kay and Bob Bivens and Missy Floyd, and my dear friend Eileen McGrady who saved my life.

For the love of my new brothers and sisters in Christ that have embraced me and share in my new-found freedom, especially Bob Beaver, John and Mitzi Davis, The Bradshaw Family, Jordan & Amanda Post, Jim Farmer, and the entire family of God at Christian Church of San Angelo.

"Here is a trustworthy saying that deserves full acceptance: Christ Jesus came into the world to save sinners – of whom I am the worst. But for that very reason I was shown mercy so that in me, the worst of sinners, Christ Jesus might display his unlimited patience as an example for those who would believe on him and receive eternal life."
1 Timothy 1: 15-16 (NIV)

Introduction

Most of my life, I viewed myself through the lens of victimhood. That is not a pretty lens through which to see life. Rose colored glasses are not much better, choosing to see things in ways in which they truly are not. They only make the circumstances from which you are living through or escape from worse by giving them more power than they deserve.

Hello, my name is Steve. That statement is one I've had to say thousands of times in my life, but it never gets old. It was hard at first to try and tell this story, exposing myself this way, laying bare the flaws and misdeeds that have plagued my life, but each time I share a part of me and shine a light on the past it makes the present so much clearer and brighter. Having spent decades hiding who I was only made me hate myself more.

It took a lot of love for me to realize that God never forgot who I was. He knows my name, He knows my story and He calls me His own. My past, my failure is not what defines me, it's what defines His love for me. The love of a father that never let go and always, always is by my side; even in the darkness, Jesus is the road builder; each time I made a bad turn in my life, he made a road back.

My life looks like a maze when you see it from above, but He knew how I would make it out and He showed me the way. In this book, I hope you will see how God walked with me all throughout my life. I was a troubled soul that He called his own, and even though this is a difficult story to tell, it's one that I hope will show you the redemption of God, his love for me and for all of us.

God is real, He is alive, and He dwells within me, and if you are a Christian, He dwells within you too.

Having doubts and problems does not rule Him out, but unless we ask for His help and truly seek Him, we will wander aimlessly along, and we will hide our light from the world and from ourselves. *Out of The Shadows* is about redemption, and I hope you are inspired to see God for who He is and embrace the friend in Christ that will never let you down. John 3:16 (NAS) says,

> *"For God so loved the world, that he gave his only begotten Son, that whoever believes in Him shall not perish, but have eternal life."*

Praise God, He chose me!

The stories herein are not easy ones to tell or easy for some to read. My life became one racked with sin. I hope that by reading this you realize that God loves everyone. He created mankind and because He created us, He loves us. How can The Father not love His children? But just because you love someone does not mean you agree with them or condone their behavior.

In the L.G.B.T. world, the motto, "Love is Love" is intended to define any love as valid and good, and any rejection of said ideas as homophobic. The one thing I have learned, if nothing else, is that love is love, and sin is sin. One cannot love God and love sin. I spent a lifetime trying to find love, and it was beside me all the time. I just never opened my eyes to see it. I was wandering in the dark seeking my own path, and that path didn't bring me peace, it brought me sorrow. Out of the ashes of my life, God has redeemed me with his love. I no longer have to search for love or friendship.

My response to God's love is simply as the song says,

> **"I am yours. Not because of what I've done but because of who you are. Not because of who I am, but because of what you've done. I am yours!"**

Let me state that whenever possible the names of the people in this book have been changed to protect the identity of others. I want to make one thing clear: I am not here to condemn anyone who disagrees with me or is still living a gay lifestyle. That is not my job. I am simply sharing with you the journey of my life and the revelations that God has shown me.

I cannot say what is right or wrong for anyone else, I can only say what I have discovered, and what God has shown me about myself and how being gay affected my life. I can say that He showed me that I have a choice in everything I do from the moment I wake up until the moment I go to sleep and from birth to death I am constantly making choices that impact my life. If the story of my life and the struggles that I have overcome speak to you, then it is not me but God that is talking to you through me in this story.

I can say that how I see my life now and the decision to "come out" as gay was a choice that was mine to make, and I was the only one that could make the choice to walk away from gay life and embrace peace once more. The struggle for most people in doing this is that the choice to walk away is not the choice most people want to make.

Choosing to do what feels good and pleases you is about choosing feelings, which as my father always said, you can't trust your feelings. The problem with trusting your feelings is that they will deceive you if you don't watch out. This is a story about being deceived and discovering that I had a choice to rediscover God's purpose for my life.

I don't apologize for being gay. I choose to walk away, and I choose to follow God where he leads me. This journey has been arduous, and I have left a trail of tears along the way. In many ways, I had become shipwrecked. Gay life for me was a remote island of my life, and I have now left the island!

Jesus is the Way Maker, and the Rescuer of the lost. He is the path that leads to freedom. In John 14:6 (NLT), Jesus said,

> *"I am the way the truth and the life. No one can come to the Father except through me."*

STEVEN STEHLE

CHAPTER I

FRIENDLESS

Losing oneself isn't something that happens overnight … it happens gradually like sand through an hourglass. The pieces of yourself gradually slip away before you realize you are no longer the you that you once were. My life has been like an hourglass, sometimes full and seemingly endless, and at other times it has seemed to be running out and almost over.

Time is elusive in that way; you think you have so much of it until you don't. When you are young you can't wait for something to happen. You have plans you look forward to, like birthdays, Christmas, and school vacations. They are all little pieces of time, that from a child's perspective, take so long to go from one to the other.

Most things in childhood are about learning: learning how to spell, how to write your name, how to tell time, etc. Learning how to manage time is a lifelong lesson, although most children have no concept of what that lesson is teaching them.

To a child growing up in the 1970's, time management was a foreign concept. The closest thing I recall about time was how long it seemed to take to get through a day of school. Public school in West Texas in the 1970's in my hometown of Midland was nothing short of torture many days.

My first-grade teacher at Rusk Elementary was Mrs. Black. I remember that even then I thought she was old. She was probably in her early sixties, which seems very young to me now as I am closely inching my way to that time in my life. I remember very few people other than family from that time in my life, but I do remember the ones that left scars on me. The first such person was Ted.

Ted sat next to me in Mrs. Black's class. Ted and I were friends, at least as much as I knew how to be friends at seven-years old. He is the first person I ever recall thinking of as my friend. I didn't have many friends growing up for many reasons but that is a totally different subject we will deal with later on.

Ted and I were both skinny little boys with blonde hair and we both liked to talk. I could be a very shy child at times, but Ted and I really seemed to hit it off.

The first conflict in our friendship occurred in that first-grade class with Mrs. Black. I don't recall the exact circumstances. I don't know if we were taking a quiz or it was just other studying going on, but I do remember what happened. Ted was talking. I don't recall who he was talking to, but Mrs. Black thought it was me.

I tried to defend myself, but to no avail. She didn't believe me, and Ted didn't admit that it was his fault. Mrs. Black was a strict disciplinarian, and in those days corporal punishment was not only allowed, it was actually encouraged.

"Spare the rod and spoil the child," was the motto that most of the adults lived by. The punishment was painful. She made me place my hands flat on my desk and she wacked me with a wooden ruler, which was her preferred form of punishment. I had done nothing wrong, but that didn't matter.

I remember thinking Ted had done me wrong and I was mad at him, It would take a while for Ted to get his comeuppance, but fate has a way of righting some wrongs. When we get to witness this, it is bittersweet.

It took two years for Ted to finally get his comeuppance. You see, Ted's mother was another teacher in our elementary school. She taught art class. Ted's mother was a very nice lady. She reminded me of June Cleaver from *Leave it to Beaver*, and in many ways, Ted was a lot like the Beaver.

One day in class in third grade, Ted was finally caught misbehaving. This time he didn't get the whack across the hands like I did; instead, the teacher in our history class made Ted get up and leave class and go and tell his mother what he had done. He was humiliated, and on top of that, he also got licks from his mom in the hallway outside her class in front of all her students.

It wasn't the revenge I had hoped for Ted to receive. I wanted him to admit he lied when I told Mrs. Black it was Ted talking and not me, and for Ted to get his hands whacked, too. But his punishment was far more than that. He got the snickers and chiding laughter of classmates making fun of him.

I will never forget how sad that made me feel for Ted. I guess I never really wanted Ted to get in trouble; I just wanted Ted to be my friend and stand beside me, but instead, he let me down. I was quite hurt by that. My first friend had turned on me. My Judas was named Ted.

Grade school was full of painful moments like that. Being shy, I didn't always speak up for myself and by the time I did, it was sometimes too late. I was one of those children that had a small bladder. That got me into lots of trouble my whole life, but none more so than in school.

We didn't have bathrooms in our classrooms. There was one boys' bathroom for all six grades at Rusk Elementary. It was located in the breezeway between the music class and the lunchroom. I often forgot to go to the bathroom during the day between classes and that caused me to have emergencies. Most of the time, I was ashamed to ask to leave class because the teachers didn't like anyone to leave class.

The results were terrifying for a young child. I would raise my hand

and ask to go to the bathroom but would be denied permission. As I sat in my seat with mounting urgency, my terror would grow and grow until the fateful moment when I would be sitting in a puddle, facing the wrath of my teachers and the humiliating laughter of my classmates.

I was bullied a lot by the other boys. I didn't know what it was about me that caused them to bully me, but they did. Looking back, my tendency to pee my pants certainly didn't help.

At home I was taught to turn the other cheek; that was Jesus's commandment, or at least, that was how it was explained to me. I turned the other cheek a lot. It didn't make me popular - it made me an outcast and a target.

Being skinny and shy, and having a tendency to cry and wet myself, definitely made me a target. I tried to explain that to my folks, but they just seemed to ignore the problem.

The truth is more likely that they had no idea how to deal with me. You see, my folks had just become Born Again Christians at that time; they were on fire for Jesus, and Jesus was all they seemed to focus on. My dad was a quiet man who didn't seem to show much emotion, but when he spoke of Jesus, he was full of Christian Fire.

I am sure my folks just expected me to get filled with the Holy Ghost, be on fire for Jesus and all my problems would work themselves out. Unfortunately, it didn't work out that way for me.

I knew about Jesus, and I had accepted him in my heart. I recall the day when I was seven-years old standing in the pew at a little Baptist Church and feeling the call to come down front and give my life to Jesus. My dad went with me and held my hand as I confessed to being a sinner and asked Jesus to be my Lord and Savior.

He was proud of me, I could tell; I don't recall many moments when I was young that I sensed his pride for me, but that day I knew he was proud of me. A week or so later I was baptized. I remember the water was cold and I was afraid, but I had seen many people baptized and as far as I could tell, no one had died from it. At least that was what I told myself.

The only thing that had to die to was sin. I didn't know how to do it, but I was willing to, or at least I thought I was.

I survived the water, my sins had been forgiven and I was a new creature in the eyes of God; but on the inside, I still felt alone. It's funny… I wasn't really alone, but I was lonely most of my life.

My sister was born when I was three years old. I loved her to pieces, but she was less than enthusiastic about her big brother. Stacie was solitary and independent in a way I had never been able to be. She made friends easily and people liked her even if she didn't particularly like them.

That was the big difference between us - she was sure of herself and unafraid of most things. I was just the opposite, and I knew it. So did she! It would take many years for me and my sister to become real friends.

I suppose for all the difficulty it took for me to make friends as a child, the one thing I am most thankful for as an adult is the friendship with my sister; my weakness and insecurity didn't always allow me to feel that bond of friendship with Stacie or any other child. My childhood was bleak from my vantage point.

The only joy of friendship I seemed to really have was my grandparents on my dad's side. Grandmother and Papa were my whole world. When I was with them, I felt loved ... especially by my grandmother.

Grandmother understood me. I think she knew I needed a friend and that my life at home was less than happy. Grandmother and Papa lived three blocks from our house. After school my sister would have her neighbor friends to play with, and I usually went to my grandparents when they were in town. I always felt loved, special, and wanted when I was with them. When I was at home, I felt out of place and alone. That feeling of being alone and out of place would take decades for me to shake.

Today as I write this, I look back over the odyssey of my life, at the friends I have made and the friends I have lost. I realize that it only takes one friend to make you feel loved and valued. That one friend sometimes changes as one takes another's place along the way.

Others that might have appeared to be friends but were only too quick to jump ship, like rats fleeing a sinking wreck. My life would become a wreck and it would take more than the love that my family or friends could provide to help me put the pieces of it back together.

It would take the love of God, my one true friend that never fails me. But at the time I thought I still was in control.

CHAPTER II

LESSONS FROM A BAD EDUCATION

Public School in West Texas was much different in the 1970s and 1980s from today. The world still believed in God. We had prayer in class and at school events. In elementary school, we started the day with the Pledge of Allegiance, and we had honor guards that were responsible for raising the flag on school grounds each morning. I remember it was an honor to have flag duty. It made me proud to be an American.

It seemed like anything big that happened in our lives happened at school. I remember all the children going to the nurse's station, with all of us standing in line to get our measles vaccine and for vision tests.

I remember watching the *Apollo Fourteen* moon walk on TV at school. It was a special program and I remember being amazed by the fact that Alan Shepard had commanded a spaceship to the moon. I must have been too young to remember the *Apollo Eleven* and *Apollo Twelve* missions, but *Apollo Fourteen* got my attention.

Seeing our American flag flying on the moon made me proud! It made me want to be an honor guard and get to raise the flag each day at school.

Elementary school was a difficult time for me, and likely made more difficult by my early childhood lesson to turn the other cheek and allow others to bully me. Our school principal was an old fat man. His name was Mr. Humphries. Today, he would be called a wussy or worse because he was such a wimp of a man. He was an effeminate man whose wife was a bull of a woman. She seemed to be more of a man than he appeared to be. The man didn't seem to have much of a backbone, and he proved it on many occasions.

One day in third grade during recess a tomboy named Shelley decided she was going to beat me up. I ran of course! What else could a sissy boy who turned the other cheek at every insult do? She finally cornered me at the baseball diamond between the baseball field fence and I was toast. She pushed me and called me names and dared me to fight, but she was a girl. I wouldn't know how to fight if she had been a boy.

Eventually, she kicked me in the shins, and I kicked her back. I think I surprised her. Of course, that got the teacher's attention and we both got sent to the principal's office. Mr. Humphries sat in his chair like a toad. He wanted us both to tell him what happened, and for once I didn't cry. I said nothing and Shelley said nothing, so he said, "Well, then, you both are getting licks."

Mr. Humphries was angry with us, and instead of trying to resolve a problem he got mad and hit us. He wasn't strong and insightful; he was weak and tried to dominate us with his authority. I saw through this but was powerless at the time. We each got three licks.

From then on, Shelley never was mean to me. Looking back at it now, she may have had a crush on me, but I only had one girl I wanted for a girlfriend and that was Pam. I remember thinking Pam was the prettiest girl in school. She had long blonde hair, she twirled a baton and could hula hoop.

Pam could have cared less about me, but I was smitten with her for years. I secretly wanted Pam to be my girlfriend but that never happened. In third grade, girlfriends and boyfriends are just things kids call each other. You hang out on the monkey bars together and pass notes in class. It's all very sweet and innocent, at least in 1973 it was. That is how two kids who like each other showed affection for one another.

Kids at that age understand love in the *philia* form of love, the bond of friendship, or at least I did. As far as matters of love and hormones, none of that was going on. It was just the age-old saga of children learning how to become friends.

My first girlfriend in grade school was Nora. She was a sweet, shy kind of girl with freckles, as I recall. She was kind and she liked me. One day, in fifth grade I think, I was with Nora on the monkey bars. While I was hanging upside down and showing off for her, I slipped and fell to the ground and broke my left arm. It was tragic. I had been trying to get attention, and I got it but not the right way.

The school nurse called my mother and she picked me up. I was taken to the hospital where they x-rayed my arm. It was a green limb fracture, meaning it had not broken in two, just split. There was no orthopedic doctor available to see me on a Friday afternoon, so the hospital put me in a splint, wrapped the arm with ace bandages, placed it in a sling, and sent us home. I was to see the orthopedic doctor the following Monday.

This could not have come at a worse time. My family had plans to go to Roswell, New Mexico to see other families in the shepherding movement of the late seventies and eighties, a non-denominational charismatic movement of Christian discipleship.

When my father got off work at five o'clock, we packed up the car and made the six-hour drive to Roswell. It was the 1970's, and the speed limit was still fifty-five, not seventy-five like it is today. It was a long drive, and as we drove my arm became more and more sore.

The pain was something I would have to endure all weekend until we got back to Midland. I had always looked forward to these trips, getting to play with other boys, the sleepovers, sharing bunk beds and just being kids. The trips to Roswell were always fun for my sister and me. We had a place we fit in, but this time was different.

I was in pain by the time we left the emergency room in Midland, but instead of staying home we kept the plans my family had made. I remember sleeping on a pallet of blankets on the floor with my arm above my head to keep from rolling over on it. That was a painful experience, one that I probably should not have had to endure, but we did not slow down or change plans and allow me to stay behind and rest. Our plans were set, and they would not change for me. I recall feeling unimportant, that I did not matter. That feeling was one that would follow me many times in my life.

When we finally made it back to Midland, I saw the Orthopedic doctor. He wrapped my arm in a fiberglass cast so the healing could finally begin, and it did. I remember being disappointed that I didn't get a solid cast, one made out of plaster that everyone could sign, like the ones I had seen on other kids.

Those looked cool! Everyone wanted to sign your cast, then you would be able to show off the list of friends that you had that said all kinds of funny things. It's really hard to write on fiberglass mesh, even if it's been heated to seal it. Once again, I felt let down, first by my parent's decision to travel, and secondly by my cast. It made me different, again, and I was disappointed once more. It is sad for me to now realize I put so much stock in being popular and wanting to be liked by other people.

Growing up I was skinny and weak. I had little to no athletic ability. I was always the kid that was last to be picked for any team, for dodgeball or any other childhood game. Even as a young man in church activities, like playing volleyball or softball, I was last to be picked. That feeling of being last and of not being valued adds to one's insecurity and leaves an imprint, one that can cause one to make choices to fit in that they might not otherwise make.

Every year, during physical education class from fourth to sixth grade we had to run a mile. A seven-minute mile was the goal for all kids. As you can imagine that is not always possible for every child. Some children's home lives included athletic activity, but mine did not involve any particular athleticism. I was always one of the last to finish the mile. It was four times around the school yard.

Coach Jackson stood there with his whistle, and he would yell at all of us to pick up the pace. He would call us names, sissy being one he used often, and he cursed. He was the first man I had ever met that used foul language. If the whole class failed to run the mile in seven minutes, he would force the whole class to run another mile, each time trying to make us reach his set timing for running a mile. It was torture, not character building.

I was scared of him. We lived on a corner and coach Jackson lived directly behind my house on the street that ran beside our house. The one boy in our neighborhood that I was somewhat friends with was Ronny. He lived directly across the street from Coach Jackson.

One day, Ronny and I were playing in his front yard, and we saw a fight between the coach and his wife. The Jackson's were going through a divorce, and they were having a tug of war over their daughter. They were yelling at one another. It was the first time I had ever witnessed domestic violence, and it was right in front of me.

In the midst of it, Mrs. Jackson saw Ronny and me. She yelled at the coach that we were her witnesses, and that she was going to tell the court what he had done. Coach was mad as hell, and I could tell. He was a mean man. I knew I had to get home as quickly as possible. I ran across the street. As I did, Coach drove out of his driveway and sped down the street, right towards me. He tried to run me over, and it put fear into me, more fear of anyone than I had ever known.

The next day at school he was lunchroom monitor. He came up to me, and when he approached me, I knew he was coming for me. I could feel the fear welling up inside of me. He grabbed my shoulders and whispered to me, "You better not say anything about what you saw yesterday. Understood?" It was a threat, and I knew he had power over me. I was afraid of him for quite some time.

Each year we would have to run the mile again and I was reminded of his cruelty. The last such experience was when I was in sixth grade. Coach had made us run the mile twice because not everyone finished in seven minutes the first time. It was exhausting. When we were finishing the second mile, he barked at us and was chewing us out, telling us we had to run a third mile.

I had had it. I had finally reached my boiling point with this tormenter. I said no, I would not run another mile. He was furious. I was standing up to him, something no one else ever did. He ordered me to do it. I said I would not, and he could not make me. He shouted something. I turned and said, "I'm not afraid of you! I know what you did, and I'll tell if you try anything".

I turned, left the field, and walked home. It was mid-day at school, so my mother was surprised to see me home early. I explained what had happened and what a bully he was to us all. She went to the school and confronted the principal Mr. Humphries. But he did nothing. He was afraid of Coach Jackson too. However, that moment of defiance, of finally not turning the other cheek, had given me some courage! It was something I would need more of in later battles. Coach Jackson never bothered me again.

I had a few good teachers at Rusk Elementary. Our history and government teacher was my favorite teacher, other than the music teacher. Music class was fun. We got to dance in class - modern dance, not ballroom dancing. I understood modern dance. I could do it. It was just like dancing at the Pentecostal church, like at Pastor Billy Van Zant's church, swaying and jumping for joy and moving back and forth. The Pentecostal dance was a lot like the modern dance of the club scene, and I was good at it … or at least the music teacher said I was.

In those days, we moved from class to class throughout the day, and for fourth, fifth and sixth grade we had math for our last class of the day. The teacher, Ms. Toney, was a big, butch woman. She was built more like a man than a woman, and she was mean. She had a big wooden paddle with holes in it that sat on her desk or hung on the wall next to the chalkboard. Most of us children got licks a time or two from her. She loved to tease her students with threats. She tried to instill fear and obedience.

Each year, on the last day of school, at the end of class, she would call names by rows or by last name letters. For example, everyone with a last name that started with 'B', would stand up when she called their name. That kid would run out the door and try not to get hit as she swung her paddle or a yard stick. If you were quick enough and ducked, you might only get hit slightly, or not at all. Most everyone got out without being too badly hit, but you watched as your classmates ran for their lives knowing that at some point it would be your turn.

During our fifth and sixth grade year, she was gone for part of it. I believe she had cancer and was away being treated. When she came back, she was changed. She had missed us. It seemed she loved us, but she didn't know how to show it. In her twisted mind, sending us off each year with a lick was her kind of end-of-school, birthday, one-to-grow-on lick. We feared her, and I could tell she didn't have many friends. Her ability to create fear was her way of having a connection that appeared to be missing in her life. I would guess looking back at it now, she had probably been abused, and this abuse was the only form of love she understood.

CHAPTER III
ROOTS

The 1970's to me were the era of Elvis Presley, hippies and "Free Love", Nixon, Watergate and the Civil Rights movement. I recall that in 1976, the movie *Roots* came out and it was a very big deal. The movie dealt with an extremely uncomfortable time in the history of the world and the United States in particular. Slavery is a very sensitive subject to talk about, but it was all that we talked about at the time. Other hot topics of the seventies included free love and homosexuality, something I did not quite understand at the time, but images of Woodstock and hippies on the campuses of universities were all things I remember from that time.

I remember watching the movie Roots. It is a very moving saga, and it brings to life the humanity of man and the degradation one group of people can inflict on another. I remember watching it and realizing that it was black people selling Africans to slave traders – Africans selling Africans - and thinking to myself how angry these people should be at their fellow Africans for having kidnapped and sold them into slavery. *Tribal Bondage:* the subrogation of one's own kind for profit, or *Racial Bondage*: the subrogation of one race or group of people for the benefit of a very select few. Both are a very nasty business.

Not all slavery of mankind takes the same form as it did in this movie. Slavery and bondage take many forms. We may all be born free men, but over time we often lose much of that freedom through self-bondage. We become slaves to self. In a way, we are selling ourselves into bondage to sin, often times without our knowledge of the chains this sin places on our life.

Satan is a master at creating slaves. In John 8:34 (NAS), Jesus says,

> *"Truly, truly, I say to you, everyone who practices sin is a slave to sin."*

As a young child of probably nine or ten years old, a kind of exploration began. I didn't have what you would call "normal" friendships, where you met a kid at school or Cub Scouts and formed a lifelong bond. My so-called friends were always the children of my parents' friends, and those friendships only lasted as long as my parents' friendships with the other parents lasted.

One such group of children were all related by blood, or group. My parents had become involved in a group of fellow born again Christians that met in home groups. We would go from town to town and visit these people. The adults would be involved in their pursuit of enlightenment and the children were encouraged to play together. I liked having other boys to play with as I had no real friends that were boys. I was all in, and happy to do whatever I could to be a part of the gang.

Sleepovers were quite common, and boys shared a bed or sleeping bag depending on the situation. My childhood sexual exploration within this group involved three male cousins from one family, and eventually two other boys from the group. I became obsessed with the naughty pleasure I had found in these experiences and would seek out the same thing over and over again with these boys. Some would participate for many years to come.

One of the boys and I got caught once by our fathers, and it scared me a little, but not enough to stop. That same boy and I would continue to seek each other out, and for both of us this would lead us down some very dark paths in our future. I don't know if he will ever escape the pain it has inflicted in his life. He seems to have tried to escape the darkness and shame with drugs, and it has been devastating for him as well. I can only hope he one day finds a road out of the pain and back to life.

I didn't know what a homosexual was when I was a small child, but I knew it was bad and that God did not approve of homosexuals. This was made very clear to me in my young life due to the preaching from the pulpit. I did not know what it meant to be a homosexual until I was probably twelve or thirteen, but I had been called a sissy boy, fag, and gay since grade school. I wasn't sure what that meant in the beginning. I just knew it was bad, and it was mean when other kids called me names.

It wasn't until I was in seventh grade that the whole thing finally made sense to me. By then I was aware of other boys' bodies, and I was ashamed of mine. Shame has a way of eating at you, and you do not even know it. Shame is condemnation that someone or something places on you…a condemnation that you don't know how to remove when you are young.

In 1977, my family and several other families that my parents were in a spiritual relationship with went to Kansas City for a worldwide Christian Convention. There were big rallies at the Kansas City Chiefs stadium. Christian leaders from all over the world had come, and it was an awesome experience to see that many believers and to hear from legends like Corey Ten Boom and so many others. The Von Trapp family (from the *Sound of Music*) sang. It was something for a young man my age to witness these sights, sounds and experiences.

Yet, the one that I will never forget was when we rode down an elevator in our hotel. There were several people, my folks included, in the elevator. On one floor the elevator opened up and a group of drag queens came onto the elevator. My dad told me not to look, but my eyes had already seen something. I knew by the way my father spoke to me that this was bad. I didn't know that they were gay, only that whatever was going on was bad.

As luck would have it, there was a huge gay pride event going on in Kansas City as well. I believe it was the beginning of "gay pride" in America. What I saw in that elevator was strange, exotic, and taboo...all things that the devil would use. He was growing his tentacles in my life, and that was fertilizer. The roots of homosexuality in my life had just been given some fertilizer to grow on.

I didn't think of myself as a homosexual growing up. All I knew was that I was different. At least I thought I was different. I did not fit in easily into any particular group of kids. The only friends I had made any kind of bonds with were kids that were children of the people my folks knew, and they did not provide friendship. It was more of a forced friendship that would not stand the test of time.

I was learning about sex and still trying to be a good little boy. I tried to be a normal adolescent, dating when it was possible to get a girl to pay me any attention. Being shy and not having the social advantages of some of my peers, I often ended up dating misfits like myself. Dating in junior high was awkward to say the least. Everyone's hormones were raging and even a confused young man like myself was trying to figure out girls.

The idea of dating boys was not a concept that I knew existed in those days. In my eighth-grade year, I was followed home by a younger Hispanic boy from seventh grade. It was about a half mile from the school to home. I was walking home, and this boy followed me and taunted me, calling me names. I would run a little ahead trying to get away from him. He finally chased me into a vacant field about a block from my house. He forced me on the ground and tried to make me perform oral sex. I was really frightened, but somehow was able to fight back enough to get away. He gave chase and finally let me go but not before letting me know he would be back for me.

I ran home and cried. My mother wanted to find him, but I barely knew his name. Looking back on it now, I realize he grew up poor, and he probably had older boys or other males that abused him. He was acting out what he knew. He was filled with rage and wanted to do to me what had been done to him.

But the fear I felt brought the only sword I had at my disposal to mind: I rebuked him in Jesus' name. That is the only clear thing about the way it ended that I recall. I called upon Jesus' name, to rescue me, and He did.

I tried to put the event out of my mind as much as I could. I was frightened at that moment, and I didn't want to do what this boy wanted, or to be gay. But the next time the devil opened the door to it I would willingly walk through it, asking for trouble, seeking pleasure on my terms. Pleasure can be just as intoxicating as a drug.

 As I entered into my teen years, there were several situations that presented same-sex experiences. The one that sticks out the most occurred when I was fifteen, I think. I was working, delivering oil field maps after school. I don't recall the date, but I recall what happened like it was yesterday. Once again, I was at an elevator waiting for it to arrive. While I was waiting, a man in his late twenties appeared beside me. My "*gaydar*", as it's called, went off for the first time. It's that feeling of sameness that one can detect in another.

This man asked if I knew where the men's room was, and I pointed. Then it happened. I followed him in, and my full taste of the power of sexual attraction or lust or just desire, whichever it was, came over me, and I wanted what I knew he was offering.

Afterwards, I was shaken. The man saw me on the street another day and stopped me. He wanted my number. This time I was afraid. I knew what had happened was wrong, and I didn't want to see him again. I panicked.

I didn't know what to do so I gave him the phone number to my dad's office at home. That office is where he conducted the church business and prayed with people, and it was not a place that I would do anything wrong. It always felt sacred to me. In a way, I think I probably wanted to get caught, so that I could tell my parents what had happened and get rid of the shame.

As it happened, he called one day. I answered the phone and fear gripped me. I had to tell my parents. They were angry with me for good reason, but they really wanted to find this guy to deal with him. They never did find him, and he never bothered me again. I met with a young-adults pastor, and he tried to explain that some of the things I was doing in my own personal life were bad for me.

You see, by this time I was masturbating daily. It consumed me, more so than most adolescent boys, I think. For me, it was needed daily. It was a drug to me; I just didn't know it at the time. I tried to work on improving myself, but I was trying to do it alone. I wasn't spiritually aware enough to be able to seek the Lord for help in these kinds of situations. I saw God as more of a rescuer, someone that in times of trouble I called upon. But not in times of weakness.

Somehow, in all the experiences up until when I left home, I still had my parents' protection to keep me from much harm. As I grew older and started making decisions on my own, my choices were not always seen by my family. I was slowly deciding what kind of person I wanted to be whether I knew it or not.

Deception was a part of me. It had been from a very young age, and it would continue to be a problem from which I have struggled my entire life. As I see it now, deception is not something you can control once you unleash it. It has a hold on you. You have to find a way to break its hold on you, so that you take each circumstance in hand, and with God's help you do the right thing.

Leaving home and going to college for the short time I was at school only opened more doors to me. I discovered more and more sex, both with girls and guys. My first experience of having sex with a girl makes me sick to think of it now. Not because it was a girl but because of the circumstances.

It was my freshman year, and the fraternities at school were looking for new pledges. Lots of beer was provided to get you interested in joining these fraternities, and the particular fraternity I was considering pledging was no exception. Older girls that were somehow associated with the Frat were encouraged to have sex with the pledge candidates.

There were two girls that were roommates who were part of that business. I gave myself to one of these women and lost my virginity to a woman. What sickens me most about that experience is what she said afterwards. She and her roommate had a bet to see who could sleep with one hundred guys first that semester. I was number twenty-five for her.

I would be sick in many ways from that day on throughout the rest of the semester. It appeared she had given me hepatitis, and it was misdiagnosed by the campus clinic doctor. Looking back, I can't believe how little I valued myself and how little these girls valued themselves. Sex was a game, a commodity and conquest. It would become that for me, too, later in life.

Starting off in college I was dating girls. I was normal, as normal as I knew how to be, but God was not in the equation. I had put Him on a shelf for now. Then one night, one of the boys I hung out with and I were drinking, and I was wasted. Before I knew it, he had taken advantage of me and tried to rape me. I was scared and got away.

He tried to keep getting my attention. A door had once again opened, and I didn't know how to shut it. That experience led to more, and by the end of the year, I was out of school and living on my own. I had failed my classes and was on academic suspension, whatever that meant. Being the first in my family to attend college, I was not prepared and had no support group.

My life was slowly becoming unmanageable, but I still felt like I was in control. By this time, I had my first boyfriend. Before long I would go to my first gay bar. That experience would be one that stuck with me for decades…my first glimpse of gay life.

From my decades of conversations with other gay men and women, gay life often starts out with some form of deception. Trying to hide who you are seeing and what they mean to you; where you've been, what you've seen, what tempts you and pulls you in that is outside the bounds of what's considered normal behavior. With what is not normal behavior, trying to find a way to coexist with others makes for a difficult experience in life, one often filled with many half-truths to try and keep the peace or avoid suspicion.

These things only tend to make you weaker and allow the roots of deception to dig deeper into your life. I was one of these people. I was good at telling lies or being sneaky. It was something that the older I got the more deceptive I became. This game I was playing would lead me down some dark roads many times.

The roots of drug addiction in my life started in 1984. That year I went away to college at Angelo State University. As freshmen, we were all required to live in the dorms. My dorm was in the men's high rise, and it was a shared suite comprised of two rooms with a shared bath. It was cramped quarters for sure and something I had never experienced before. I was the first to arrive and my roommate-to-be was my high school buddy, Rusty, who didn't arrive until a day or so later.

In the adjoining suite was another young man, Martin, from some place in central Texas. That night I smoked pot from a bong made out of a coke can. Martin had brought the weed with him, and I was eager to join in to feel like one of the guys. However, bad decisions just take one step to get you going down a road that leads to destruction. The first root of drug addiction had been planted, and it would lead to much worse over time.

There had been other addictive behavior in my life already, so drugs had an easy root to my soul. Having an addictive personality doesn't always present itself until later in life. Mine started in adolescence with sexual behavior and exploration. I'm sure some exploration is normal for all children, but I was consumed with it once introduced. Pleasure was my weakness, and I was on a slow road of destruction in search of pleasure. I just didn't know it.

The summer of 2020 marked forty years since that chance encounter in Wall Towers West in Midland, Texas. I was just fifteen years old the first time my *"gaydar"* went off, that thing inside of me that recognized another homosexual man. I had a choice to follow that spirit, and I made my first conscience choice to act out as a homosexual. I was coming out from under the protective covering of my parents, and I knew what I was doing was wrong. It was seedy, and it was a door that I opened that day which would take decades to realize what I had done.

In hindsight, it's very clear how wrong it was, and that I was being influenced by an evil spirit. It wasn't a "gaydar". It was this evil spirit within me that knows the principles of God's law, that recognized a like-spirit that is outside of God's law that would do me harm. Spiritually and emotionally healthy men do not instinctually choose to go after homosexual encounters; they reel from them.

That thing inside of me that knew that it was wrong was the Holy Spirit. It has taken me forty years to understand that the spark inside me that goes off is God's way of telling me to beware. God's law is written on my heart, and the Holy Spirit inside me is saying, "Beware my child. This is not good for you."

I have noticed it more and more these days, and so I am aware that it is God talking to me, not the other way around. If God, Who loves me, has written his law on my heart, then I know it instinctively, and that is how I see God warning me to, "Beware my child."

I have also realized that once I have established a relationship with another person there is no longer a reaction, unless another evil spirit manifests itself that I am not familiar with, or I have not allowed the evil spirit to operate within me. This proves in my mind that "gaydar" is not some magic power to detect gay people. If it were, then it would go off every time any gay man sees another gay man, and so on and so on. It would not happen as a warning and then leave once it's done its job. That is exactly how the experience happens…it surfaces, and then is gone until needed to reveal the truth again.

Romans 2:14 -15 (NIV) says,

> *"Indeed when Gentiles, who do not have the law, do by nature things required by the law, they are a law for themselves, even though they do not have the law, since they show that the requirements of the law are written on their hearts and consciences also bearing witness, and their thoughts now accusing, now even defending them."*

CHAPTER IV

THE FIRST TIME I CAME OUT OF THE CLOSET

In 1985, my parents had seen enough signs to know I was probably involved in gay relationships. They had grown concerned after having come to visit me and spending the night with me. I lived in a rather large one-bedroom apartment across the tracks and across the river. This was the barrio, but it was what I could afford.

The place had character. The apartment was the back half of a two-story house, and it had a big, screened porch that faced the river and the tracks with a koi pond out back. The inside had a big kitchen, a decent size living room, and a stairway to nowhere along with a bedroom and bath. You had to cross over the landing of the stairway to nowhere from the living room to the bedroom going up and down steps. The quirkiness gave it a little charm it would not otherwise have had.

The night my folks visited I slept on the couch, and my folks had the bedroom. Late that night, around two a.m. in the morning, the phone rang. In those days, we only had landlines, and my phone was in the bedroom. My mom answered it and called me to the phone. I was still half asleep, so I didn't realize what was really going on at that moment.

The call was from my first boyfriend, Doug. I had not heard from him in a month, so it was completely out of the blue. As my folks lay in my bed, my ex-boyfriend and I had a fight. It was obvious to my parents that there was a guy on the other line and that this was some kind of lover's tiff.

After I hung up, I was suddenly aware of my surroundings. It was like waking from a bad dream and realizing other people have been woken up by your cries in the night. I don't remember how I explained it to my folks, but I made up some lie and hoped they would buy it. The storm had passed for the moment. I thought I had survived it without anyone asking any real questions, but that was just the calm before the battle for my life.

 A few months later I got a call from my folks making me an offer: an offer of money and position, a way to make a career. My father ran a small printing company as his day job, but his real job was pastor of a small congregation. My folks offered to give me the printing business and pay me more than I was making at the bank, and I could save money and live at home.

The carrot had been offered, and I tried to resist but I could not. Money was the driving force. I didn't think I was going to be allowed back to school, so this was a way to be successful, or so it seemed. I moved home and worked for my dad, but my every action was closely observed, even more so than I realized.

About the same time, I had found out that my dad's first cousin, Glenn, had moved back to Midland. He had a big house not far from us. I knew Glenn was gay and I wanted to be a part of his world. He lived in a big house that sported an indoor pool with a waterfall, a very mid-century Frank Lloyd Wright kind of house. and I loved architecture.

I came up with an idea of how to get his attention. I would give him a "welcome-to-town" gift, a bottle of champagne. That would do it, but when I went to his house he was not there. Another man answered the door. I would later learn that this man was his partner. I left the bottle and explained who I was.

A few days later Glenn called the house, but my mom was the one that answered the phone. He had called to thank me for the gift. That was the spark, the one that would set things ablaze. "Why were you trying to see Glenn?" she demanded to know. "He is not welcome in our home." He was an outcast as far as my folks were concerned.

The next day, or the next week, I'm not sure exactly, but shortly after the Glenn incident, mom started asking questions. "Who is this person named David that always calls you? How do you know him? Is he gay? What about Doug? Is he gay?"

Then it happened - my moment had come. As my mother and I sat arguing about my friends, I finally said it. "Yes, they are gay, and I am too! Are you happy now?" I was angry that she had forced me to say it out loud.

My father was in his office with the door open while all this was going on. He heard it all and was furious. In his anger, he said to me I was no longer his son. He wrote me a check for five-hundred dollars, fired me, and kicked me out of the house.

At that moment, my grandparents came to the office. They never usually came to the office, but they had decided to stop by. They had always been the kind of people that would just stop by. They had entered into a hornet's nest. My dad in his anger said, "Tell them! Tell them what you told us."

I told them that I was gay, and the reaction was not what I expected. My grandfather said, "Well I knew this guy in the army. And old Mr. Johnson…" the man that had the farm next to theirs, he was gay and lived with his sister. I was shocked! My grandparents, my dad's own parents, knew of other gay people.

My Grandmother, who had always been my protector, said, "Well he's coming to live with us. Let's go and pack your things." So that afternoon, I moved into my grandparents' guest room. It was the same room I had spent my childhood days in. It was safe there.

My grandparents showed me love, not rejection. They didn't

approve of homosexuality. Of that I was certain, but I was still their boy. My grandparents used to say they had three boys: Murry, Garry and Steve. I was theirs, and they were not going to give up on me that easily.

My grandmother tried to convince me that I would never be happy living this way. She loved me and wanted me to be happy, and she was afraid of what this might do to my life. The AIDS epidemic was in full swing. We were just learning of the "Gay Cancer" that was killing people. My grandmother didn't want me to get AIDS.

I don't recall what exactly occurred to bring back the peace with my folks, but after a while, a month or so later, I was welcomed back home, and moved back in with my parents.

I was back in church and going to the youth fellowship. I had tried to straighten up my life, but my eyes had been opened to the gay world, and it was all around me. The calm would not last long. I secretly made new gay friends, and I was sneaking around trying to avoid being caught.

On New Year's Eve, 1985, our family was to go to a New Year's Eve service at the church. It was a covered dish event where the adults would pray in the new year. I had other plans for that night, and it would take a big lie to get away with it. I claimed to be sick and stayed home. I had made plans to move out that night.

I had a new friend, named Mark, that I was planning to move in with. Once the family was safely gone, I called Mark and he came over. The two of us moved all my belongings out of my bedroom. I had made a break for it. I don't recall if I left a note or just vanished, but it was done. My sister came back early to check on me. She found my empty room and informed my folks, and in turn, the whole church that I had left while they had gathered.

In the following months to come, I had many adventures. I attended the Super Bowl in New Orleans, seats on the fifty-yard line, all expenses paid vacation with dinner at Brennan's. Mark was trying to buy my affection, but I was not interested in him. I had met someone in Dallas, an older man named Jack at JR's Bar and Grill.

Jack made me feel special. He plied me with drugs. The first time I took ecstasy was with him. It was still legal to buy, in fact, the bartenders sold it from the cash register. Soon, I had moved from Mark's to my cousin Glenn's, and then to Dallas with my new, much older boyfriend, Jack.

He was controlling me, or I was allowing him to, and I didn't even see it. I was all alone at his apartment, in Irving, far away from the gay night life of downtown Dallas. He had been to Woodstock and had lots of druggie friends. Even his boss did drugs with us. He didn't want me to work, and once I was dependent on him, he told me we were moving to San Francisco. He was an executive with HUD, and he had been promoted to a new position.

While he was at work, I packed the apartment for our move. Just before we moved, he informed me that my father had found out where he worked and had called him. He was afraid of my dad and told me to tell my dad to leave him alone. Apparently, my father had threatened to try and expose him as gay and get him fired. I called and told my dad to leave us alone, but I could tell he was hurting. I could tell by the conversation; his heart was hurting for me. He told me that if I ever needed him all I had to do was call.

We drove cross country from Dallas to San Francisco via Las Vegas. Jack had friends we could stay with in Vegas. The night in Vegas was memorable to say the least! He took me to a famous Italian restaurant where all kinds of Hollywood types hung out. The atmosphere was just like *The Godfather*, with people coming up to each other and making grand gestures. "Oh, it's been so long since I've seen you. How are you doing, how's the wife and kids, and who's the cutie you're with?" That kind of thing.

It was a big place, and we were seated in a booth on one side of the room. In the middle of the room across from us was a long table with probably ten or fifteen people at it. At the head of the table was an older man who I recognized. I had seen him on T.V. my whole life. This man's character on T.V. was an idol of mine. He was confident and manly and was the kind of guy I only wished I could be, a James Bond type, but from a different crime show drama.

This man noticed me, little ol' me, and he asked the waiter to have me come to his table. I was in shock and in awe! He was famous and

I could not believe he wanted to meet me. The waiter brought a chair and sat it next to him. He offered me a glass of champagne. It was his fifty-fifth birthday, and this was his party. He had a young, new wife with a baby about eighteen-months old, and his grown, teenage kids from his first marriage showed up just then to wish him a happy birthday. My idol, a married man, was groping me under the tablecloth. He was gay!

I was shocked that he was doing these things to me in front of other people that might have noticed. I got nervous and said I had to get back to my table. One California idol had fallen, and we had only made it to Vegas. The tale of this Hollywood Star would give me a story to boast about for many years to come.

San Francisco was exotic and wild, and I could tell it could be dangerous. While my boyfriend was busy getting settled into his new job, I explored the city. One day, I ventured into a leather bar. It was mid-day, but there were guys walking around with nothing on but boots and a hat. I saw things that I had never even imagined existed. This was dangerous territory, and my young mind knew it. I began to get concerned I had made a bad decision to come to California.

Once we had moved from the luxury of a hotel suite paid for by the government to a small one bedroom furnished apartment with twin beds, this person I had considered my boyfriend informed me that I would need to get a job and pay my way. He was no longer interested in me romantically. He just wanted a roommate in California since he didn't know anyone and didn't want to move alone. He had used me. It was obvious. This upset me, and all my silly plans were falling apart.

One evening while I was sleeping, I had a dream. In the dream, I was falling off a cliff and above me was my father. He had thrown me a rope, and I was holding on to the end of it. The rope had a knot in it, and I was holding on for dear life. It was a vision about my future, one that I was certain I understood. The next day I called my father. I told him I wanted to come home. We had only had a few conversations here and there keeping in touch, but he was on a plane the next day.

Dad came and saved me. He didn't judge me. He was thankful to have me back. He told me of all the people that had been praying for me, and about one person in particular, Tracy, a girl from youth group at church. She had prayed for my return, and she was interested in me.

I didn't realize she had those kinds of feelings for me. To be honest, my life up until the time I left the church was so chaotic. I was living in two different worlds, and I wasn't fully a part of either of them. Things did not make sense to me until I left California.

The drive back with my father was good. As we talked, he let me know how scared he had been for me, that God had a purpose for my life, and that all of this could just be forgotten in time. I shared with my dad the dream I had about falling. He told me that God had shown me my life and that it was possible for me to lose my life. The choice I made to call him was the lifeline that had been offered. God was showing me I had a choice.

CHAPTER V

BOOM! I'M STRAIGHT

Upon my return to Midland, I was welcomed back with open, but somewhat skeptical, arms. I was thrust into many aspects of family and church life. My sister was engaged to be married, and Tracy and I had started seeing each other outside of youth fellowship. I was determined to get on with my life and put the past in the past.

I liked Tracy. She was very attractive, and we got along pretty well. She came from a large family, and she was the oldest just like me. Tracy also had a past that she was trying to escape from. She had a son, the cutest little boy I had ever seen, Jason. I recall one of the first times I saw Jason, he was probably 18 months old. I think I fell in love with the idea of being Jason's dad as much as I did the idea of marrying Tracy.

Things moved very fast for us. I was in a hurry to put the past behind me. I think Tracy wanted out of her parents' house to change the way she was viewed as an unwed mother as much as I wanted to change my circumstances. That doesn't mean it was easy. My father had arranged for a group of elders of the church to meet with me and to try and cast out the spirit of homosexuality within me through deliverance. I didn't say it at the time, but I was just going along with them. Whatever it took to get them to accept me. I wanted for it to be over, but I didn't think anything had changed. I simply said yes and agreed to what was going on.

I had made a choice to be straight, and that was enough for me. I was doing it all on my own strength. For the moment, it was all going as planned.

Within three months of moving back, I was engaged to marry Tracy. I remember the night I asked her to marry me the first time. She said she would have to think about it. Several weeks went by and we had gone to a party with some of her friends. When we got out of the car she said, "Oh, by the way, yes." I had no idea what she meant, I said, "Yes, what?" It had been so long, and I'd forgotten the question. That was just the beginning of our crazy courtship.

Asking Tracy's father for her hand in marriage was one of the more intimidating things I have ever done. It was like going on the biggest job interview I had ever had…only the person doing the interviewing doesn't like you, they don't trust you, and they know they probably can't keep you from marrying their daughter. Tracy's father had one stipulation: before she could marry me, I would have to have an AIDS test. In my little town, my sins were known, and to many they were stains that would never be washed away it seemed.

The Midland County Health Department didn't seem to agree. I was told they didn't think I needed one. I had to fill out an application, explain all my past sexual behavior and why I thought I needed a test. The man that interviewed me told me I was not a high enough risk to get tested; that I had not been "gay" enough; I had not had a blood transfusion, and I was not an intravenous drug user. It would take quite some pleading with this man to test me.

The county didn't want to spend the money, and in 1986, the county was the only one testing. Eventually, I was able to get them to test me, and to my relief, I was negative.

Tracy had told me she wanted an unusual ring. She did not want a diamond; she wanted a sapphire for the stone. When I went to see Mr. Jenkins, our family jeweler, he talked me out of a sapphire. He said I could not afford a true sapphire, that my budget would only pay for a chemically treated stone, and that my betrothed deserved a real stone. He sold me a nice round diamond set in a Tiffany style mount.

I was excited. Our wedding plans had already begun, as it was May of 1986, and we were to marry in September of 1986. Things had begun to get a little stressful between us. I'm sure the wedding caused Tracy lots of stress. Her mother and mine both had lots of ideas and very little time to get things done.

Finally, one afternoon I convinced Tracy to go for a ride. I wanted to give her the ring. Things could not have gone worse. I had planned for us to go to a park by my house; I would get down on one knee and ask her again with the ring. The whole romantic movie moment, but that never happened. The weather was a bit rainy, and she didn't want to get out of the car.

Tracy was frustrated and was complaining about the wedding. Why did I bring her here? It got heated, and I got mad. In my anger, I threw the ring box at her and said, "I'm trying to pop the question, but you're being a bitch!" Things were not starting out good! Things didn't get much better when she saw the ring, either. It was a diamond and in a traditional setting. I tried to explain what the jeweler had said. I explained that she could pick any mounting she wanted, I just wanted my ring on her finger before my sister's wedding.

In hindsight, I was pretty darn foolish and selfish, but Tracy didn't help matters much at all. The one thing I know now, is that if you truly love someone, that love is more important than the ring. Jewelry is just an ornament, and a pretty ring will not a happy marriage make.

CHAPTER VI
ROCKY ROADS AND SHIFTY SAND

In many ways, our marriage was over before it began. We did not have a solid footing. Jesus was not the tie that bound us to one another, and we started falling apart before we even got married. We had promised our families that we would wait until marriage for sex. Well, that didn't happen. I can say the blame lies with me; I didn't hold my own self in check.

Before we were wed, I would also do drugs again. One night on a date, a friend said he could get some acid, and I decided to do it. Tracy's folks were out of town, and we invited the group back to her folks' house. To say it went badly is putting it mildly. I had a very bad acid trip. I saw alligators on the walls, and everything was creepy crawly.

That was the last time I would do acid, but not the last time I would do drugs, for sure. That night probably created even more problems for me. I had opened a door again that would take decades to shut.

Times were tough, economically, in Midland in 1986. I had tried for six months to find a full-time job but couldn't find one. Eventually, I found a job in Garland, Texas, a suburb of Dallas, for MBank Centerville. I had an uncle that lived in Plano, north of Dallas, and I could stay with his family until I found an apartment for Tracy and our new family once we were married.

Before we even got married, I had faced my first temptations. The first such time was the first night in Dallas. I went to JR's Bar and Grill on Cedar Springs. I could not help being drawn to it. I was drinking and soaking up the gay atmosphere, knowing I was supposed to be at my uncle's. By the time I arrived late that evening in Plano, all hell had broken loose. Tracy had been calling all evening trying to reach me. When I called her all she did was wail, crying and screaming that Hoby was dead. Her uncle Hoby who was about ten years older had died tragically in a car wreck. She wanted me back in Midland. I don't recall what excuse I gave to her or my family as to why I had not arrived on time in Plano.

Tracy's family grieved heavily, something I had never seen before. In my family, death was sad, but we always seemed to know that it was just a new beginning. Tracy's family took no such comfort from this that I could tell. It would not be the last time I had to hold her and try to comfort her in such circumstances.

Dallas was going to be trouble for me if I didn't get my act together quickly. I found that out soon after I started the new job. The bank I worked for had hired a temp for a couple of weeks. He was gay and we hit it off immediately. Before I knew it, I was close to crossing the line with him. I had to really reel myself back in quickly. If I didn't, I feared it would all end badly.

I straightened myself up, pulled myself back together, and proceeded with the wedding plans. I don't know when I had the thought, but it had occurred to me that if it all didn't work out, I could always get a divorce. I was thinking of ending it before it began.

The day before the wedding I flew back to Midland. I must have looked like I was frightened because I can recall my father saying to me on the way back from the airport, "You don't have to do this. It's not too late to call it off."

It's not too late, he says. Are you kidding me! Now you tell me I have a choice? But I was determined I was going to do things my way.

I wasn't prepared for marriage in any way, shape, or form. I had been going ninety miles an hour trying to escape my past and had not found the time to prepare myself. I certainly had not made God a real part of my life. I was doing my best to put on the mask that everyone wanted me to wear.

The one thing I was most excited about was being a dad. I loved Jason. He was a sweet little boy with a smile that could melt your heart. Tracy and I didn't waste any time trying to have more children. We wanted to make a real family, and I loved the idea of kids. Jason turned three years old a month after we got married, and before the end of the next year our son Jaret was born.

Jaret's birth was the most exciting thing that I had ever experienced. Birth is amazing, watching his little life grow inside Tracy. The anticipation of another child is something that I will never get over. Jaret was born with strength. He looked like a linebacker. I couldn't believe he was my kid! I was such a skinny guy. I barely weighed one hundred twenty-five pounds when Jaret was born, so to see such a brute of a boy that bore my name was amazing.

We were now a family of four. For the moment, things looked like they would only get better, but if I could screw things up, I would. Before long, I was unemployed. I had gotten caught with my hands in the till at work. I was a very stupid man. I had a job as the office manager for a department store, and I was in charge of opening up in-store charge accounts. It wasn't long before I devised a plan where I could create an extra charge account for myself under my dead grandmother's name.

This was a nice store that had designer clothes, and I wanted the best for Tracy. I was trying to buy her affection with things. I had a little system going that I could keep up only for so long, and it eventually caught up with me. My employers must have felt sorry for me; either that, or they just wanted to save face that they hadn't caught me until

I had been at it for several months. This was not the first time I had left a job in disgrace, and Tracy had to deal with the consequences. Having to come clean to Tracy was worse than dealing with my employer. I don't know why she didn't leave me then and there, but she didn't.

Before long, God had a new plan for us. I found a job that would provide me a career for decades. A family friend of both our parents was needing a guy to train. It was a great opportunity, and we took it. There were all kinds of promises from this man for advancement. I was very excited. He was a Christian, and his father-in-law was a pastor of a large church in the Dallas area. Both our families had ties to his family through church organizations. I was hired and I was a great fit. I understood the information intuitively as if God had designed me for this purpose.

With the new job, we would have to move again either to Big Spring or Midland, and since we both had family and friends in Midland, we chose Midland. Not long after moving, our daughter, Jade, would be born. I was a very happy man. Jade was a joy, and I loved having a daughter. When she was born, I was the first to hold her since Tracy was under sedation. I was able to carry her in my arms from the delivery room to the nursery. The nurses handed her to me, and it was love at first sight. I will never get over the feeling of that moment. It was a magical one that I thought could not be broken.

I worked for this man for three years, and after many broken promises, watching him get wealthy while my salary stayed the same, building his business from just himself, me, and a part time secretary working out of his house to a large operation with many employees while I was the one training them, and my pay didn't change, I finally stood up for myself.

I had been approached by another man who owned a larger company that offered me $100 more a day and a real chance for a job with benefits if I liked working for him. The man that had given me my start was furious. I had tried several times to get a raise. He would promise raises and bonuses, but he always failed to provide them while I watched him pay off his mansion and buy new cars and a second home for his family.

To say I was jealous and disappointed, was putting it mildly. In hindsight, I had done some really bad things in other jobs where I had been given lots of opportunities and I had blown them, so maybe this was just settling the score. But my sense of entitlement would be something I would have to battle for many more years.

At the new job, I started out as a contract employee and then was offered a full-time job with benefits. It was a dream come true. It seemed that this new job gave my little family more stability, but it would also require me to travel a lot more. Traveling would put lots of stress on my marriage. I did not know how to handle stress, and in the stress, I chose to seek escape.

I would drink most nights when I was out of town. That would lead to me purchasing porn magazines and then movies in the hotels. It was a downhill slide into self-indulgence and pleasure. It was an escape from the frustrations of home and a wife that was angry I was gone so much. This, in turn, would lead me down a road that I would not be able to return from for several decades.

One night while I was working out of town in Ozona, Texas, I was staying at one of those hotels built around an indoor pool, hot tub, and sauna. In those days, it was called a Holidome hotel since Holiday Inn was the first to have a Holidome that included such amenities. I had a bottle of Jack Daniels and was in the hot tub alone when a very handsome man about my age came walking past me.

He headed to the steam room. I thought about following but decided against it. In fact, I had been searching for just such an experience for weeks at this hotel and now that it was here, I got cold feet. Steam rooms are notorious meeting places for gay men. After a bit, he came out of the steam room and got into the hot tub. He was cordial, and we chatted. His name was David, and he was on his way to San Antonio to see doctors at the Air Force Base. He had been wounded in Desert Storm in Iraq.

He was a warrior, a fantasy come true. I don't know how it happened, but he started playing footsies with me, and it just went on from there. I was shocked, I guess, and a little intoxicated for certain. I was weak, that was certain too. By night's end, I experienced a romantic passion that I had never known before. Sex didn't occur, but I was smitten. He was dangerous, and I was a mouse he had just toyed with.

The next day we had plans to meet up. I was so consumed with this man I had just met that I could not make it through the first part of the day and went back to the hotel just before noon. I had to see him, but he was gone. I was beside myself. I was a wreck all over someone I had barely met and didn't really know anything about.

I checked with the front desk. He had left me a message. He had to leave early, he told me his schedule had changed, and told me how to reach him. I was destroyed. I don't know what I thought I was doing. All I knew was that he had awoken feelings in me that I had never known. He had shown me pleasure without sex that was so intoxicating that it lingered for days.

I wanted him, and I was at a crossroads in my life. I knew I could not call Tracy and tell her what was going on. She would be furious. I also didn't know what to do about my feelings.

I decided to call my friend Lance. I told him everything. He listened and gave me some advice. Lance said I would have to choose. I could not keep going on like this. If I was going to try and be with this man, I would need to get a divorce. He said it's not fair to Tracy for you to do this, so you have to choose, and I did. I chose to be sneaky and see where things went with this guy.

Before all of this happened, a small change in my relationship with

Tracy occurred. In the year or so before, she had gotten reacquainted with a friend of hers from high school that turned out to be a lesbian and whose brother was a world-famous chef. This woman and Tracy started reconnecting, and I didn't have much of a problem with it.

I wanted to go to her brothers' restaurant in Dallas. I was cool with a high school buddy of hers that was a lesbian, but at about the same time, my friend Lance had come out of the closet to me. It was no shocker to me or to Tracy. He had been the best man at our wedding. He was twenty-nine, single, and had only ever been on one date with a girl in his life. That was with my sister, and that didn't work out.

When Lance came out of the closet Tracy forbade him from coming around and forbade me from having anything to do with him. I was furious. He was a lifelong friend, and I couldn't turn my back on him because he was gay. Also, what about her friend? Well, there was a double standard for lesbians it seemed. She could have her gay friend, but I could not.

The following weeks or months were filled with lots of frustration and deception on my part. I was trying to make sure I could guarantee a future with David before I left Tracy.

Well, as they say, the best laid plans are laid to waste, and mine were. On the way home from a family trip to see my parents, Tracy and I had been fighting in the car. There were mean things that we were saying to each other in front of our kids. The conflict was obvious, and I remember trying to end it. Then, Tracy turned to the kids and said, "If mommy and daddy get a divorce, who do you want to live with?" I was stunned she would say that to them. Our son Jaret, being the smarty pants he was like his father, said, "Neither of you!" He was hurt. I'm sure the fight was hard for the kids to watch. They all loved us, and we were destroying their world.

In time, things came to a head with Tracy, and I had no choice as I could see it. I wanted out, and I thought I had planned it all perfectly. Boy, was I wrong about that! At first, I let Tracy think it was another woman, but then she became suspicious, and she accused me of being gay again.

I had worked hard not to let her or anyone else know about the gay thing this time. That didn't work. She was convinced, and I was mad she was pointing the finger at me. That next day I think I moved out. I moved into Lance's guest room until I could get an apartment.

Both our families got involved. Once the cat was out of the bag, it went nuclear. It's funny now writing this that I say nuclear. A nuclear bomb wipes out everything in its path. It destroys everything leaving a scorched earth. That is how things went with our divorce.

CHAPTER VII

ANOTHER LOST BATTLE

The divorce was becoming messy. During spring break of 1993, I took my children on my weekend with them to my parents to stay for a week. Things had been very strained with my folks, and I chose to leave after I dropped the kids off. I could not stand the heat as they say.

I went back to San Angelo for the weekend and partied with a new gay friend I had met. I didn't check on the kids because I felt they were in good hands with my parents. When I returned to work on Monday morning, I was stunned to get a call from Child Protective Services. They demanded I come down and temporarily sign my rights away or be arrested.

I had no idea what was going on, but it appeared that someone had accused me or someone I knew of having abused my daughter sexually. I was freaking out. It was preposterous to me! To think that anyone I knew could do such a thing, and I knew I didn't do anything. I was surprised to find out who was saying that this happened and then it came out. It was my own mother.

The night I had dropped the kids off my mom noticed, while giving Jade a bath, that Jade had some mild irritation on her upper thighs close to her private area. My mom asked a two-year-old, "What is that?" To which Jade replied, "That's where man bite me." At least, that's what my mom thought she heard her say. Then came the questions. "What man?" "The man with red hair."

These were the words my mother believed she heard from my two-year-old and they got repeated over and over again. It would later be proven to be false by Child Protective Services, but not before my life and the lives of my children were destroyed. To this day, I don't believe anything happened. I certainly hope it did not. But with Child Protective Services involved, everyone was trying to point the finger at someone that could have done what was being claimed.

All I do know is that Jade was bit by red ants in the sand box at the park where the boys practiced soccer earlier that week. I had the kids every Wednesday and every other weekend, and I had allowed Jade and Jaret to play in the sand box close to the soccer field while I watched Jason practice. Jaret came and got me because Jade was crying. She had been stung on her upper thigh by ants.

I held her and calmed her down as best I could. We left the park and went to Walgreen's where I bought her some cream for the sting. When I took her back home to her mother, I gave Tracy the ointment and explained what had happened. That was Wednesday, and by Friday evening all hell would break loose.

Fear has a way of controlling situations, and it did for my parents, and for Tracy as well. My parents didn't call me and ask me anything. They didn't trust me at this point. They could only think the worst and reacted accordingly. When I called my dad asking what had happened after getting the threats from Child Protective Services that Monday morning, he told me that they had brought the kids back to Tracy and that their attorney had advised them not to talk to me.

I was in shock. Shock is putting it mildly. My world was caving in, and I had no one to turn to. Child Protective Services was going to arrest me unless I gave my kids up. It would be a mess, and I would lose my job. I was in the fight for my life, and I was losing the battle in miles, not inches!

The next few weeks and months were a blur. I could not see my kids. I didn't know if anyone had actually harmed my daughter. I was looking for answers and getting none. Things came to a bitter end when I was told that Tracy, her folks, and my folks wanted me to give the kids up. They wanted me to just walk away from my children.

Through an attorney, I was told that if I did that Tracy would not tell my boss and I could keep my job. I had a choice: fight, be exposed, and still probably lose, or I could save myself and go along with what I was asked to do. I called my grandfather who was the only family member still talking to me. He was furious with my father, and said that if it was him, he would just walk away and never look back. Forget the Stehle's. I again was at a crossroads that I had no idea how to navigate.

Tracy and her mother had promised that if I signed my rights away, I would still be allowed to see the kids under their supervision. It was the only loophole I saw that gave me a glimmer of hope. It was to be short lived. My attorney was not much help. She was only in it for the money and didn't have anyone's best interests at heart. All she wanted was her two-thousand five hundred dollars and to be done with me.

My three friends - Lance, Reece, and T.J. - went with me to the attorney's office to be by my side as I did the wretched thing of signing away my parental rights. The papers had been drawn up. I was a wreck.

That would be the hardest thing I had ever done. Afterwards, I fell apart. I sobbed for hours. It was a death, but not just one death. It was like three deaths at once… I had just lost everything!

On August 4th, 1993, on my grandmother's birthday, Tracy filed a letter with the court saying she had requested I terminate my rights. I held on to that letter hoping it would prove I had not chosen to abandon my kids. I felt it was my ace in the hole, but in hindsight there was no ace in the hole. I had made a decision: I chose myself and my future over fighting for my children's future.

As the divorce proceeded, I kept things under wraps at work. For the moment, no one knew what was going on. It was still private. The divorce hearing kept being rescheduled, and Tracy's attorney seemed to be up to some tricks.

When we finally had a date for trial it was in the County Municipal Court, not the District Court. I wondered about it myself at the time and brought it up to my attorney's partner who was representing me that day. He didn't know how they got it changed from District to Municipal Court, but we moved forward anyway. I hadn't changed my mind. At this point, I still had a choice, but I wanted it over. It was draining. I had lost everything, and this was just the nails being hammered into my coffin, as it were.

At the trial, it was just the Judge, the court reporter, Tracy, me, and the attorneys. When the judge asked if I knew what I was doing by signing my rights away I said I did. He asked if I was coerced into doing this. I lied and said no. He then had Tracy testify to the facts of the case and asked the attorneys why I was giving my rights up. Tracy's attorney said that it was because I was gay, and Judge Fitzgerald without skipping a beat said, "Well, I would have taken them away anyway."

I knew then I was done for. Not even the court was impartial. My life as a dad had come to an end.

Immediately after the divorce was granted, Tracy broke her word to me. She marched from the courthouse right to my boss's office and told him everything! I walked into the office as she was exiting his office with a smirk on her face, laughing as she walked out. My boss, Wes, called me into his office. He immediately cut my salary by ten-thousand dollars.

On August 6, 1993, two days after Tracy filed the letter with the court, Child Protective Services issued a letter that they had closed my case and that they had concluded that nothing had happened. It had been "ruled out." But it would not arrive in the mail until after the divorce was final. It appeared that the letter was held for mailing until the divorce was final, as I received it only after all documents had been signed and the divorce was final. The case had been concluded earlier, but the information was withheld from me.

The father of one of the kids on Jason's soccer team was the man that was in charge of the case at Child Protective Services. There had been collusion to make sure I fell in line and terminated my rights. The date of our divorce hearing had been moved from August 8 to September 8, and on September 8, 1993, my life was forever changed by these choices and decisions.

There are many choices I would change if I could go back and do it over, but that is not possible. The only person that can make something good out of all my bad choices is God. He is the righter of wrongs and the healer of hurts. Without his grace and forgiveness,

I would not have been able to survive. Because of the pain that this caused I did almost everything imaginable to end my life many times through drugs.

True to her word Tracy agreed to let me see the kids on Christmas Day, 1993. I went to Tracy's parents' house and had Christmas with the kids. Tracy was still allowing me to speak to the kids on the phone. I had spoken to them several times, but this was the first time I had seen them in over six months.

By then, my life had moved on, too. I had a new partner that I was living with already. I met Lee in the evening on the day of my divorce. That was also our first Christmas together as a couple.

I didn't stick around very long with the kids. I guess I thought there would be other days. Because I had to spend this time with Tracy's folks, who at this point made me feel like I was less than dirt, it was a difficult day. The kids were not happy, and I was not happy being left with Tracy's mom to be my chaperone and having to listen to her questions.

This woman had worked hard to remove me from my kids' lives, and now I was having to spend time with her. I had nothing but hatred for this woman. I am not sure how long I was at my ex-in-laws' house that day, but I believe it was about an hour after Tracy left me with them to join her new boyfriend, Ross.

I made the choice to leave. It's another decision I would come to regret. Apparently, I didn't spend the appropriate amount of time with my kids, and I had failed some test I didn't know I was taking. When I called later that day and the next to talk with the kids, I was told no. Tracy and her mother had decided I was not worthy of talking to them anymore and that I could not see them either. The promise to allow me to see the kids if I signed my rights away would not stand. They had chosen to end it.

The truth of the matter is I failed my children. I chose my own path based on my own selfish desires. These same desires had managed to control me, so much so that I chose myself over my family.

Yes, things were rough with Tracy, and yes, I quit on us. This, in part, is because I did not have a real relationship with Christ. He was just a savior that I called my own but didn't have any connection to other than by his choice to call me as His own. I had spent my life living as an outcast, barely living, when He had already called me as His own. My wrong thinking has cost me dearly in this life.

Christmas of 1993 was the last time I ever spent with my children as kids.

CHAPTER VIII
STARTING OVER

Somehow, I moved on. I didn't know how, but I remember thinking that somehow it would all change one day. I kept thinking that since I had that letter from Tracy and her mom giving me proof that it was not my idea to give the kids up, and because Tracy and her mother had signed a letter requesting me to give them up in exchange for limited visits, that my proof would someday show I had not just walked away without a care.

That gave me some hope, I guess. There had not been one day that I had not thought about my children since I left my family. I had failed them, and I didn't know how I could ever make it right again.

Shortly after our divorce, Tracy married Ross. She wasn't single for more than six months. She had moved on, too. One evening after they were married, I was leaving Albertsons, our local grocery store. I saw Ross's white truck parked right out in front of the door. Tracy was in the front seat and Jaret was in the back. He saw me and started waving. He was yelling, "Daddy, Daddy!!"

Tracy placed a newspaper across the windshield to block him from seeing me. I felt then that there was no more hope. I was crushed. I lost all the strength to fix things, if that was even possible, which I did not know how it could be.

In 1995, Lee and I had plans to move to North Carolina. On the day before we left town, Tracy's mom drove up to our house. Lee and I were in the garage going through things when I saw her at the end of our driveway. I was surprised that she knew where we lived. I thought I had taken great strides to keep her and my family from knowing where I was. I had lived in fear of her ever finding me since the day she had broken into Lance's house to accuse him in the witch hunt to find a red-headed man to blame.

Somehow, I got the courage to walk down the drive to her. She was yelling at me, "Are you just going to leave town without saying goodbye to your kids?"

This made me furious. I told her she was just there trying to excuse some guilt. She knew Tracy wouldn't let me see the kids, so I asked her if she would get Tracy to let me see them. I reminded her of the agreement. Her response was "You know Tracy. She won't listen to me."

I asked her to talk to Tracy. It was a chance and one I had to try if I had any hope of ever seeing them again. I called Tracy and asked her if I could see the kids before I left town. She said she would have to talk to Ross about it, and that she would let me know the next day.

When I called the next day, she said that Ross had said no. They thought that the kids had moved on and were happy and that I would just stir things up. I did not argue or fight. I gave up once again!

Lee and I settled into our new life in Charlotte, NC. Things were so different in a big city. Gay life was not hidden like it was in West Texas. But I struggled finding a job that would pay me much money. I had been making good money in Midland. I had a trade that was valuable in Texas, but North Carolina had little to offer me.

It wasn't long before Lee was asking me to go back to Texas and work to pay off his high credit card bills so that he could afford to buy a house. Being in love, or what I thought was love, I did what I was asked to do. I moved back to Midland. I became roommates with my friend, Reece. I worked to pay off Lee's debts. Every payday, I would go to the credit union that he had loans with, and I would pay thousands of dollars towards his debts.

While I was away, Lee would find other lovers to spend his time with. Things would get tense between us. I would break up with him, and he would woo me back. It was a cycle that he was able to hold over me for seven years.

I moved from Midland to Charlotte, Charlotte to Midland, Midland to Dallas, Dallas to Charlotte, Charlotte to Dallas, Dallas to Charlotte and back to Dallas. We would break up and he would smooth talk me back. I would get angry and leave. He would pull me back.

He had a power over me, one that would take another decade from which to finally move on. His lies and deception finally caused me to see who he was. I could not trust him, and he broke my heart into pieces. After him, I would never fully trust a man again. The hurt he put me through would follow me for twenty-seven years.

Looking back at it today, I can say that God was showing me that even though I thought I was in love with Lee, that it was a false love. There was no depth to it. It was fickle. The commitment to each other was based more on sex than love. Love is patient and kind, it does not seek its own way and love endures all things.

There is no deceit in love, and the one thing that Lee was good at was lying. He was charming and charismatic, but his lying is what finally showed me the light about him.

On one of our last trips together to see his family, Lee made up a lie about having to go back to Charlotte early, when in fact, we had plans to go to New York City. I had heard him tell his mom the lie, and I just sat there and listened. The next day his mother asked me if what Lee had told her was true, if we were going back to Charlotte for the reason he said. I was cornered. Either way I was in trouble. I said yes.

He had now made me a party to his lies because I didn't want to hurt his mother, and I didn't want to create any problems in the family or in my relationship. I was now lying for him. If he could lie to his own mother about something as innocent as wanting to continue a trip to another destination, what was he capable of lying to me about?

That was the beginning of the end of us. I was beginning to see the writing on the wall. We had a fight over his obligation to help me out with my truck payment. Work was not steady for me in Charlotte, and I had sacrificed everything for him numerous times. I had paid his debts, arranged for him to buy a home without any thought to my security, as I wasn't on the deed. I had made him a prince, and now I needed his help.

Our friend, Manetta, had cosigned a loan for me, and I was behind on payments. Something had to be done. I had made an old woman get collection letters and calls. All I needed was Lee to take my needs into consideration. Not just mine but our friend, Manetta's, as well.

That didn't happen. Lee let me down again, but still I clung to him. It would all end in public humiliation that left me no choice, but for now I was still holding on, trying to right a sinking ship.

CHAPTER IX
BIRDS OF A FEATHER

"Birds of a feather stick together." This old adage tends to be true with most gay men. As a gay man, once you find one, you find another. Before you know it, you have a small flock of friends.

The bar scene in the 1980's, 1990's and early 2000's was such a group of people. My first gay bar was a little hole in the wall in San Angelo, Texas called *Phase 2*. The first night I drove up and circled the parking lot for about thirty minutes before I got the nerve to go in.

I was supposed to meet my then-boyfriend, Doug, at the bar. Doug knew about the bar, but had never been. I waited for Doug, but he never showed up. I finally gathered the strength to overcome my natural fear of the place and went in.

This was not a place anyone would recognize. There was no name on the building, just a single light with a street number on the door. It could have been anything I was walking into. There was a doorman who asked for an ID and if I knew what kind of bar this was. I said I did. I paid my cover and was buzzed into the place.

Inside was filled with cigarette smoke and the foul smell of musty carpet having had many drinks spilled on it. The place was dark. I remember that someone came up to me and said hello. His name was Bill. Bill introduced me to a group of people. We drank, smoked cigarettes, and when the song "Wake Me Up Before You Go-Go" by Wham came on we got up and danced.

Someone handed me a small bottle and told me to hold it up to my nose and inhale. It was a foul-smelling substance called Amyl Nitrate that people called poppers. It was sold under the guise of video head cleaner or room deodorizer. In many states it is banned.

This chemical made the world spin. I was warm all over, and everything started to slow down, like a slow-motion movie. It was intoxicating. I was hooked on the feeling immediately; it was pleasure. Before I knew it, there were bodies grinding against each other, some I wanted the attention from and others I did not.

By the end of the night, I was kissing some stranger I had just met and would go home with him. I would see more of him, and he would give me a sexually transmitted disease (STD) known as crabs. That should have been enough for me to say to myself, "Hey there, wait a minute, you're not a complete idiot! Slow down, turn around, think this through."

But it wasn't. Everything was about pleasure. Everyone I met was about pleasure. My existence had become based on when I could go to the bar, who I could meet, and who I could sleep with. Pleasure was my choice, and it was the only thing I cared about. I was consumed by my selfish desires of the flesh.

Over the next several months, I would bounce from guy to guy looking for some satisfaction. Each person I met was damaged goods. It was like looking for a diamond in a pile of broken glass. Some things shimmer in the light but can cut you.

With each new experience, I was slowly doing more and more damage to myself. I didn't know a good relationship from a bad one. I judged each gay man by the last, dating in secret, and to most of the world it was a secret. That is why gay people always want other gay people to come out of the closet. Once you start the process, it rips a band aid off the scars you have hidden from the world … scars of self-doubt and inner demons that are begging to come out.

For me, it was anticlimactic to come out the first time. I was not really coming out yet, just testing the waters. Each experience would tend to make me think I'm special, that they liked me, when in truth most of the men I met just wanted to use me. I was a bank to many, while to others I was just a conquest.

My first boyfriend, Doug, and I would find friendship again - if you can call it that - later on. Doug and I traveled to Dallas to go to my first real gay club where people congregated in the open, not hidden like in San Angelo. These places had names like JR's, The Old Plantation, The Mining Company, and everyone's favorite - The Round-Up.

At The Round-Up, guys two stepped together. Back then, it was enticing for me to see handsome guys decked out in cowboy boots, wranglers, and starched shirts while dancing, twirling, and having a good time. It would be a place I would go back to many times over the next several decades.

Gay men often tend to have multiple relationships within a common group of people. A guy will date one guy, and then dates another. Then, those two end up dating each other, while the first guy moves to number four, and the list goes on and on and on.

Lee, Clay, and I had such a situation. I had not met Clay, but I found out about him because I stumbled across his name when I had my suspicions about Lee and his philandering. I came across an email exchange between the two of them one night when Lee was out of town. I didn't meet Clay for some time. It wasn't until after he and Lee had been a thing, and after Lee and I had gotten back together for the last time.

When I originally found out they were seeing each other behind my back I went ballistic. It was Christmas time, and I had just put up the tree. Lee had gone out to El Paso to do a concert series, and he left his Yahoo email up. Something made me look at it.

My grandmother always said if you want to know where something is, ask Steve, he will find it, he's a snoop. She really meant I was sneaky. She would say he has probably seen it or can find it. This is true, I have a detective's ability to see things that others just pass up and don't follow through with.

When I found the emails between Lee and Clay expressing their love for each other I lost it. I decided to move out while he was out of town. I was vindictive, and I did my best to let him know how much he hurt me.

I printed out every one of the emails between them and I taped them up on the walls. I called the antique dealers and sold everything that was mine that I could not take with me, and I left the Christmas tree up but stripped of its decorations. I had found a picture of the two of them and put it in a frame. I found a pair of silver wedding bands that we had purchased, tied them together, and taped them to the picture with a note saying, "Hope they fit."

Being vindictive I did something I truly regret. It was not nice, but I rode around for three days in Lee's car with the window rolled up and smoked cigars in it. All the while, I made out like things were fine with us when I would speak to him on the phone. I could lie too!

The night he arrived back in Charlotte I was supposed to pick him up at the airport. I never showed up. He called and called my cell phone, but I just let it ring. He had no keys to the house; they were locked in his car where I left them.

When he finally made it into the house, he found it was empty except for his bedroom furniture, a sofa, a Christmas tree, and lots of emails posted on the walls. When I exacted revenge, I felt like I was a giant. I was filled with rage, rage that would fuel more things later in life.

When Lee wooed me back to Charlotte for our seventh attempt at a relationship, it was under false pretenses as well. I had once again caved to this powerful hold he had over me. I had quit my job in Dallas for the second time. The people at Hexter-Fair would ultimately give me three chances to work for them, and I would blow all of them.

I quit my job, not having any job lined up in Charlotte. Lee flew out to Dallas to help me move. We had my pickup and a U-Haul trailer loaded down with all my worldly goods. We headed to New Orleans to spend the night on our way and would stop to see my friend T.J.

Somewhere in Louisiana around the swamps of Alexandria, Lee said he had something he needed to tell me. This was ominous I could tell. He claimed he had a roommate at home, just a roommate, and his name was also Steve. It was very convenient to say the least since we both had the same name. He didn't get confused and call one of us by the wrong name.

He said that Steve number two was just a roommate, but he had not told him I was coming back so I would have to find someplace else to live until Steve number two moved out. I was furious, and I told him he was lying. Why would a roommate care if he was bringing his partner back? It didn't add up.

I was four hours from Dallas in the middle-of-nowhere-Louisiana, and he springs this on me. I had no job, no place to live, and obviously no relationship. I didn't know what to do. I was embarrassed, but he still had a hold on me. We stopped for the night in New Orleans, and I confided in my friend T.J. that things were sketchy with Lee. T.J. wasn't much help because he could not understand why I kept going back to Lee. I think he secretly hated Lee but would never say it because he had more class than that.

The next day we continued towards Charlotte. I called my friends, Tony, and Allen, and they offered me temporary accommodations at their home. They said, "It's your room, babe." They had been my rescuers several times, and they would continue to be throughout my days as a gay man.

I had no job, no home, but I had friends. Friends that could not understand why I still wanted to be with this person who put me through so much pain.

Tony and Allen were an anchor in a stormy sea of my life, the port that was always open, and they tried their best to offer me moral support and guidance. They had taken on the role of elders in my life. They were, for all intents and purposes, my closest thing to gay family.

They never judged me. They offered me shelter and a job from time to time. I would learn many things from Allen as an Interior Designer, and I gleaned much from him. He was a talented man, and I took full advantage of his tutelage.

After about a month of Lee and I meeting in secret to avoid Steve number two, the "roommate", Steve number two moved out, and Steve number one moved back in. My friends thought I was crazy, and I most definitely was. My decisions were not at all rational. I was blindly making decisions solely on my emotions; reason and faith played no part in my decision making.

Shortly after being settled in the house with Lee, we went out one night to a local gay bar to have a few drinks. On the patio, Lee saw someone he wanted me to meet. It was Clay…the same Clay that he had been seeing when I left him the last time. His words were, "I think you two will really hit it off. He's a lot like your friend T.J."

I had no desire to meet him. I still had the bitter taste of their affair in my mouth, but we sat down anyway. Somehow the conversation turned to a friend of Lee's in El Paso named David. Clay said, "Oh. How is David doing?"

I quickly noticed that Clay knew this person. I asked, "So you know David?" He replied, "Yes. I met him last year when I went to see Lee in El Paso."

I had done it. I had caught Lee in a lie for sure this time. Lee had denied all along that anything had really gone on between him and Clay, but this was proof that the affair was real. Not only that, but he had also included other people in the knowledge of it.

Beyond that, he was continuing to lie to me about his affairs. The next week I met Steve number two, who turned out to be a jilted lover as well. My relationship with Lee was built on lies, one right after another, and I was beginning to see the light. But what to do? How do you end a relationship that you can't get past? For me, it would take public humiliation.

Each year the Human Rights Campaign in Charlotte would have a big social fundraiser event. There would be hundreds of small parties around town. It was a progressive dinner type affair, and it would conclude with a big event downtown at First Union Center for dessert, dancing, and a silent auction, all to raise money for gay causes.

This was the social event of the season. The "who's who" of the Charlotte Gay Society would be there along with politicians. It was a big deal.

The evening started off badly. I could tell Lee was having another affair. I had been upset for days. He was up to his old tricks, and I knew it. I was in tears when we finally arrived at the party, but he just kept ignoring me. I was probably making a spectacle of myself in all my despair.

Towards the end of the evening, I was talking to Clay, telling him how upset I was. Clay noticed Lee walking hand in hand with some young man towards the parking garage out of the Atrium of First Union Square. Then it happened.

Clay yelled, "Lee! What are you doing? You have a husband." Husbands are what we called our partners. When Clay yelled out, it was as if you could hear a pin drop, it echoed across the building.

I was humiliated. Clay thought he was sticking up for me because we had bonded over the fact that we figured out that Lee had lied to both of us when he was dating Clay. As it appeared, Clay was innocent. He had been taken advantage of in much the same way I had, or so he would say. Now he had defended me, and at the same time, humiliated me in front of four-thousand people.

That was it. I'd had all I could stand, and so, I moved out for the last time. I actually found a decent job and was trying to move forward in Charlotte. The town, however, was poison to me. Before long, I would meet a new set of friends…ones that liked to party and do drugs. I was about to slowly set off on a journey that would nearly end my life numerous times.

All the while, Lee was trying to get me back. He was like a snake in the grass and just as deadly to me. I finally decided I could not remain in Charlotte. It was just too painful. So, I called and got my old job back in Dallas. They had hired me back for a third time.

The evening before I was to drive back to Dallas, Lee asked if we could have dinner together to say goodbye. I'm not sure why I agreed, but I did. The evening was nice. We didn't fight, and it was all very romantic to be honest. Lee could charm anyone when he wanted to.

After dinner, we went back to his house for a drink. We sat on the sofa talking, and he tried to seduce me. He was saying all the right things, and a part of me wanted to stay. But as I looked into his eyes, I said, "I'm going to do something uncharacteristic. I'm going to leave because the person I see is not the person I know. I don't know who you are, and I'm not going to be fooled anymore."

I got up and walked out. I had broken part of the curse that had bound me to him, but the pain and the regret for making him an idol would be something I would carry with me for decades.

After Lee, Clay would go on to seduce me, and he would play a role in my life for many years. This flock of people in my life would often scatter like doves in hunting season at the first shot. When my life became chaotic, they would generally scatter. The friendships were not deep, even though on the surface they would appear so. Each new friend, each new relationship would only last a little while.

Seasons came and went in my life. All the while, I never forgot about God or Him being my God. I just kept him on the back burner.

CHAPTER X
THE NIGHT THE LIGHTS WENT OUT IN GEORGIA

When I left Charlotte on my way to Dallas, I stopped in Atlanta. It was Halloween, and there were lots of dance clubs to visit. I decided I would stop off for a day or two and have some fun. Oh! How I would come to regret that decision!

I don't recall the club I was dancing at, that's all a blur to me, but I was having fun drinking and dancing. I met a few people, and I was having a good time. I met a man from the West Coast. His name was Jim, but I kept calling him Bill. The music was so loud, I thought he said Bill. We had a very nice time, then another guy cut in and Jim-Bill let me do my thing.

The new guy must have roofied me. I ended up taking him back to my hotel. I didn't even know his name, but the next morning he was there, and it was obvious he had raped me when I was unconscious. I was frightened and ashamed. It was unprotected sex with a total stranger, and I had not been aware of it.

His words have rung in my ear for twenty years. He said, "Don't worry. I'm bi-sexual." I knew in an instant that this was bad. Bi-sexual men are careless. They think they can't catch anything because they aren't gay.

All the bells and whistles in my head went off immediately. I was frightened of him and wanted him to leave. I kicked him out, and then I went to get drunk. I didn't think this could happen to me. I thought I was being safe. That was the lie I had been telling myself, but I had just allowed a perfect stranger to control me and my future.

I had reservations for another night, so like a fool I stayed that night and went out again. I didn't know anyone, and I was alone, so I went back to the same gay bar. Once again, I ran into Jim-Bill, the guy from the West Coat I had met the evening before. I could tell he was kind. We talked. I opened up to him about what had happened the night before with the stranger, and he did the kindest thing - he comforted me.

I was so worried about getting HIV from being raped. It's odd looking back that I was more concerned about the virus than the fact that I had been assaulted and raped. My fear of the virus was more concerning, but Jim listened to me.

He then revealed that he had been HIV positive for seventeen years at that point. He was the first person I had actually met that had the disease, and he wasn't dead. He was living, and he gave me hope. He was a shelter in a storm and would continue to be a friend for many years.

He is a generous kind man that would give the shirt off his back. He is a hard-working entrepreneur that has been taken advantage of by more people than I have, and that's saying a lot. Jim was the light in the darkness that God placed at just the right time for me. God knew my future, and that I would need a friend to encourage me.

Several days later, I made it to Dallas and started my job at Hexter-Fair again. I had been in Dallas for only thirty days when I was hospitalized with pneumonia. It would be the first time I would be told I was HIV positive, only to be told I was not; that I had tested as false positive. I had hope again, but I was weak, and my inner compass was broken.

The experience in Atlanta and all my failures had begun to mount up on me. I needed more and more ways to escape the demons that plagued me. Soon I was doing cocaine on a regular basis, and then a daily basis, until I finally lost my job. My boss was a kind lady, and she had tried to help me, but I kept screwing things up. Finally, she'd had enough. I had given her no choice but to fire me.

I drifted from place to place, having lost my apartment for lack of a job, spending every penny on drugs. I had also found the bath houses. I was a frequent flyer in these places. I filled every moment of my days trying to find a way to make enough money to buy drugs to go to the bath house and party with other guys.

It was depravity at its worst. I was in a bath house on September 11, 2001, when I saw the Twin Towers fall on live TV. That should have been a wakeup call. Hello! Sanity calling! Pick up!

I was at a low point in my life. My father reached out and offered me a job taking care of his father. I finally got myself cleaned up enough to go take care of my grandfather who was in failing health. This was a lifeline my father had thrown me to give me a roof over my head and an income, and all I had to do was take care of Papa.

It all sounded good to me, a clean start, but it quickly went downhill once I got there. My grandfather was in bad health. His eyesight had gone, and he was wheelchair bound by now. Taking care of him was a twenty-four hour a day job, one I thought someone else should be doing.

I was ungrateful for the opportunity to say the least. I wanted to have fun, and there was no time for fun of any kind. Every time I left the house to go to the grocery store or to the pharmacy and pick up items, my grandfather would call 911 and say he was having a heart attack. I would come home and no Papa, just an empty house, with a wheelchair turned over and an oxygen bottle laying on the ground.

It was like living in an insane asylum at times. I was depressed, and I couldn't sleep. The old man wanted to get up three times a night, and be up and fed by six a.m. Then the day would start all over again. It would be up and down and up and down. He would get angry because he couldn't see the TV. He wanted to die and asked me to kill him.

It was more than I could take. I was not prepared for this. I was a mess on my own, and I was trying to care for a man who was having end of life issues.

After several months of this, I'd had enough, and I wanted out. My dad and I had a big blow up. I was really mad at him. I felt like he should be dealing with these problems instead of me. I know I said some really mean things and may have used curse words. I was so angry. Looking back, I was already angry. It just finally came to a head, and I let it out.

When I did, I ran away just like all the other times, but this time to Florida. Clay had a big apartment overlooking Las Olas Blvd in Fort Lauderdale. I could come stay for free and find a job there. So, off to Florida I went.

CHAPTER XI

THE BEACH IS NOT MY HOME

Things in Florida started off on a good note. I met people quickly. I arrived in fall, and by Thanksgiving, I was having dinner on a five-million-dollar yacht with a bunch of people clinging to a millionaire who was a letch and an alcoholic. Not the kind of person everyone wants as their new best friend, but when you have very few friends...

My choices were not any better in Florida than in North Carolina or Texas. I was on a constant search for pleasure. I was out at the bars, nearly every night. On many occasions, I would go home with some new stranger. I was a barfly, an aging one, but I still was young enough to catch the eye of folks that looked my way and that was all that mattered.

I fed on the attention. It was a drug. My need for constant gratification and approval was enormous, one that I could not control. I did some really unsavory things to earn money. I never prostituted myself, but I sure came close.

After about three weeks I found a job. This time it was for a horrible company that did foreclosure title work for repossessions of houses. This was the worst job I can remember doing in my life. Every day I dreaded going to work there. The air was thick with misery.

This was a paper mill, and there were fifteen employees that worked foreclosures for nearly all fifty states. I had Tennessee, Mississippi, and Louisiana, along with Florida, as my states. The woman that ran the office was a former head nurse from a mental hospital, and she ran the place like a mental ward. She paced up and down the aisle of the office making sure you were working and not talking or doing anything but solid work.

Personal freedom was something that did not exist in this workplace, and I could not wait to find another job. But it paid the bills, and by now, I had a new wardrobe. One fit for the night clubs and the dance bars with the pretty men. I was finally beginning to find my way into the club scene, and that's when I met Carlos.

Carlos and I were like fire and gasoline, and once we were together it was like two rock stars entering the clubs. Carlos knew everyone, and he made sure everyone knew we were an item. Carlos was king of the clubs. He was a promoter, so he knew all the bar and club owners. He also knew who had the best drugs. We would go on to be regular members of the Ecstasy and GHB party crowd.

About six months after we met, Carlos told me about an opportunity to do a nationwide promotion for a new sports drink that had just come on the market. If we could get the job we would own our own promotion business, run the promotions, travel nationwide, and have a great time going from city to city. I quickly agreed and we got the job. Life now was Carlos twenty-four hours a day, seven days a week.

For a year, we traveled all across the country from New York to Seattle and Miami to New Orleans and every state but Alaska and Hawaii. In every town that had a gay club, we would go to party. Carlos could always score. He had connections everywhere, and where he didn't, he had the Latin network that always came through.

What I didn't realize, until I had made the decision to do this, was that Carlos would be my boss. We were not equals in this. Carlos was the front man, and I was the grunt. It was grueling work. I set up big sites of games and had lots of heavy metal pipes to move around. I somehow got to be the one to deal with the manual labor part while Carlos made new friends with the site owners and the contract talent. I was a mule, to put it bluntly.

I really don't know how I managed to do it. I already had a bad back. Lifting heavy steel pipes and heavy thick plasma T.V.'s, then hanging them on the walls of the truck were things you get a young man of twenty to do, and I was forty. This was going to end badly, and when it did it was over jealousy and frustration. I'd finally had enough of a hot Latin temper from a man that did not appreciate my knowledge of issues and who saw me as an object, like a trophy, more than a partner.

I finally called it quits. The night before we were to leave Fort Lauderdale again and head to New York I quit; I just walked out. That's how I always handled things. I just quit.

I crashed at Clay's again and started to look for a job. Clay had told me about a job at Nordstrom, and he would put in a good word for me. I went and applied. The day of the interview everything was going well. I had been offered the job and just had to take some tests that were standard new hire things.

In the middle of the tests, I received a call from my sister. I never got calls from my sister and never in the middle of the day. I answered and could tell it was bad news. It was Jonathan, my little brother. He'd been killed in Germany in an army training exercise.

I remember feeling like it should have been me that had died, not Jonathan. I was the bad child. The one that had been tossed away, the gay boy that no one loved, the fag that deserved death. That is how I saw myself and how little I loved myself. I felt sorry for myself, and I blamed myself at the same time.

This time I fell apart. I wailed and screamed. It must have really frightened the people I was with. I had gone to the atrium of the mall to be able to hear what Stacie was telling me, and I screamed, "No,

No, No, No!" Then I just fell to the ground.

The next couple of hours were a blur to me; I don't know what happened. I don't know how I got back to Fort Lauderdale or to Clay's house from Aventura Mall. It was all a blur, but I made it back to Clay's. Once the shock had worn off, I decided to do the one thing no sane human being does when a sibling dies: I went and got high. I went, found drugs, and escaped everything. I escaped into pleasure and tried to hide from my feelings and emotions. It lasted for about three days, then, I got myself back together and headed to Texas for the funeral.

My parents' friend, Conrad, had purchased a plane ticket for me to fly home. I must have looked like Liberace or Elton John getting off that little plane in San Angelo, Texas. I had on a leather bomber with beaver fur and some outrageous shirt, decked out in jewelry and who knows what else. It was obscene in hindsight, but I wanted to make a grand entrance. I wanted to show how gay I was to these people.

I was looking for a fight. I had an attitude, and I was looking for trouble. I was hoping to have a "Why are you gay? Why are you so flashy?" conversation. I wanted attention, but it didn't happen. Everyone treated me with love and respect. I was now the only son, not the other son. Things had changed, and my father and mother didn't want to lose another child. They could tell I was soon going to be lost if I went back to Florida.

STEVEN STEHLE

CHAPTER XII

AND THEN THERE WERE TWO

My brother Jonathan died a hero. He was killed in an army training exercise that cost him his life, but not before he gave his for his brothers-in-arms. Jonathan was where God wanted him to be that day. If not for him, three others would have died along with him. If they had been in battle, they would have most likely awarded him medals. I don't know if they even acknowledged the real sacrifice he gave.

My sister spent nearly a decade fighting the army to get justice for him and make sure no one else died the way he did. However, justice is slow and the pursuit of it can weigh you down more than the issue you are fighting for can. I see how the effect of my brother's death and the loss of him impacted my sister's life. She went into full momma bear mode.

Jonathan was the first child she helped raise, so she was very protective of him. His legacy was one she fought valiantly for. She was ultimately able to do some good in the end. To this day, the U.S. Army fears my sister, and that is something to be proud of!

Losing Jonathan was hard on everyone in the family, and we all processed it differently. Myself, I tried to block it out for many years with drugs and escaped into sexual depravity. I was trying to numb my senses so that I did not have to deal with the loss on any real level.

However, the loss also brought my sister and me closer together, and it increased the bond between my parents and myself. For many years, I had tried to put my family on the back burner. I was angry with them for turning their back on me. At least, that was how I saw it.

In reality, they had never left. They just didn't know what to do with me. I had become someone and something that was foreign to the person they had raised me to become. I had chosen a path that they had no understanding of personally and everything that they did know about it scared them to death.

Once I was back in Texas for Jonathan's funeral, things sort of fell back into place for that period of time. Family relationships were normal, if you can call it that. There was a peace that had come over the strain between us all.

My children needed to be informed of my brother's death. They had not had a relationship with my family for several years at this point, but he was their uncle.

In the years prior to this, Tracy and her husband had made the decision to end the relationship with my family. They felt it was too hard on the kids, and in looking at pictures from that time period, I can see how distant they were with my folks.

The strain between them was real, and it was caused by me. Tracy and Ross wanted a normal family life without the hassle of dealing with my family and the constant reminder of me. My parents agreed to the terms Tracy had set again. She had moved the bar on them, and it was to remain there for years to come.

Jonathan's death was an opening for me to see them once again. They came to the funeral with Tracy. She was there to stand guard and make sure that I didn't get too close to them. It was very evident that she despised me and wanted nothing to do with me, and still wanted to control our children's lives and their response to me.

There are lots of things I remember from that day, but the one that left the biggest impression was when my son Jaret stuck his hand out and shook hands with me. He made the move. He had the courage to take a step and we both took it. It was short but meaningful, and it would be the parting of the sea between us. We just did not know it at the time.

My brother's funeral was one of the hardest things I had ever gone through up until that time. The full military honors and the family dynamics made my life seem kind of small in comparison. The whole situation made me pull closer to the family and want to be there for them. I had a purpose, and it was good to be wanted and needed again. My family wanted me to stay in Texas, but I was determined to return to Florida. It was especially hard on my mother, but I put myself first again, as always.

I didn't have a job, but I was sure I could find one again. This time I felt empowered, like I could conquer things since I had a new-found relationship with my family. I was foolish to think that I could do everything on my own power, but that is exactly how I felt.

As soon as the situation settled down at home, I returned to Florida. I had no job or home to go back to, but with the little money I had in the bank, I found a small, one-room furnished apartment. Within a few weeks, I found a great job in West Palm Beach. It was a forty-five minute drive every morning, but I was committed.

The company was great, with good people who all seemed to like me for the most part. Particularly, one woman, Eileen, would become a friend for life. She would be responsible for saving my life in the future.

This job was one God wanted me to have. He made sure I clearly saw the good and bad in people. I saw the brokenness in people that lived for themselves and had no relationship with God. I was promoted to a good position that gave me my own office in a two-office suite away from the main team. This gave me the opportunity to spend time with the only other occupant of the suite, an older man named Billy.

In reality, Billy was only about ten years older than me, but he looked like he was thirty years older than me. Billy was a fully functioning alcoholic. This was the first time I had ever spent any time with a real alcoholic. I had known a few in my family growing up, but they were distant relatives, not someone I spent days on end with.

Billy would get to work at about seven-thirty a.m., and he would already have beer on his breath. He reeked of booze, and by eleven a.m. we would usually go to lunch together. Billy would need to drink, or he would begin to have the shakes. He needed booze to function. Lunch usually lasted two hours with Billy, but since he was my direct supervisor on that floor, what he said went.

Billy was a very kind man, talented and generous, but lost. He and his wife would spend the evenings getting hammered. It wasn't for fun or entertainment; rather, it was a lifestyle. Every day by five p.m., Billy would have his first of many gins, and then go to vodka, and later to beer. Then, he would sleep and start the next day over again with beer.

This was the life they lived. They had things that they enjoyed like cooking and baseball, but life was just passing them by. Looking back, I can see that God was testing me. He showed me with Billy how easy it was to get lost; how my life could end up the same if I continued on the path that I was going. But I still didn't see it for myself at the time.

My First Home

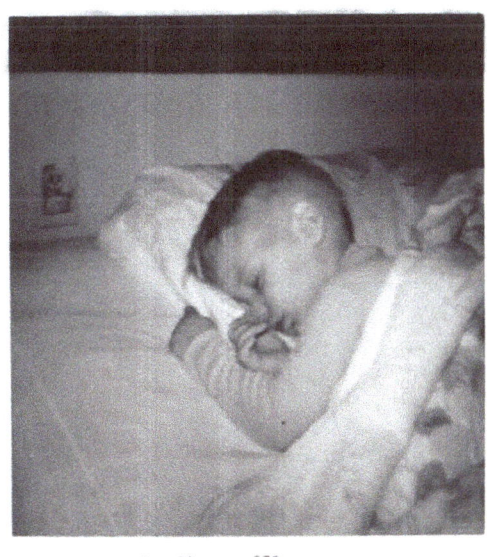

Peaceful Life

First Birthday

Christmas 1966

Me & Stacie 1967

Family 1960's

Never too old to sit in Grandmother's lap!

Grandmother & Papa, a love story

Granny Green who lived in pain her whole life

Grandmother & PaPa with Jaret

Favorite pic of Jaret, age 5

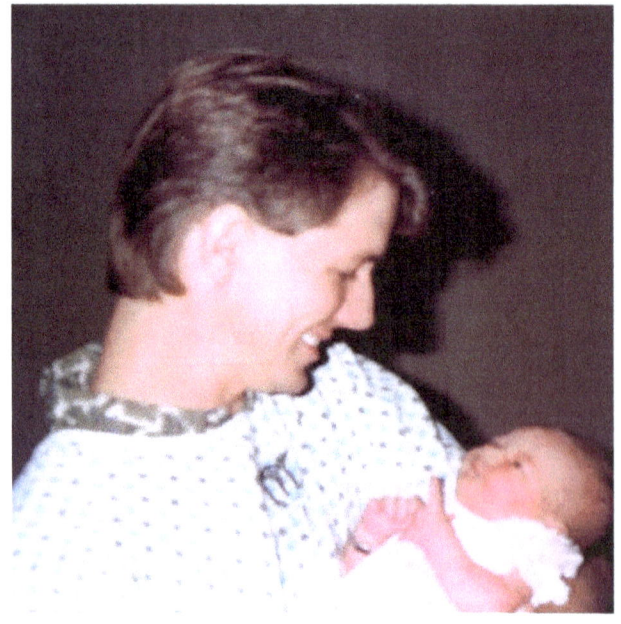

First photo of me & Jade

Mom, Dad, Stacie me and Jonathan - Denver

Mom & Dad, A True Love Story

Jonathan

Last pic of Stacie, Jon & Me, I was high on cocaine.

First picture of me & Jaret, reunited 2007

Me & Jaret

Imperial Float Pride 2001

Leather & Death

Driving myself to rehab 2018

Leaving rehab 2018, a new man

Me & Stacie

My Family - Dad & Mom, niece Callie, brother-in-law Tripp, Stacie, nephew James, me & niece Katie

CHAPTER XIII

NO LONGER NEGATIVE

Being told you have H.I.V. is a scary thing for anyone. I have been told several times that I had it, only to be told it was a false positive. One day, my boyfriend at the time, Randy, and I went to get tested. I expected everything to be fine as usual. A few weeks went by before the test results came back. I went to the clinic to get my results, and the man that was running the clinic said at first that he could not find the results. Then he said, "Oh, yeah. Here it is. Yes, you're positive. Next!"

I was just a number to this man. He didn't give me any advice or help me. He just sent me away to figure out this news on my own.

I was devastated. I remember driving back to my condo feeling like someone had just let all the air out of my lungs. I was in a fog, and I felt sorry for myself. I was headed to a dinner party with neighbors in the condo complex, and when I arrived, I sat outside in my car. I was frozen.

I kept thinking, "How are these people going to accept me?" I had begun to judge myself immediately, and expected everyone else to judge me, too. For now, it would have to be a secret, because I didn't know who I could trust with this news.

I arrived at the dinner, and the whole time I felt like I was floating, like I wasn't even there. I kept thinking, "How can these people like me? If they knew me, the real me, they would not like me." I was dirty!

Looking back on it now, I realize that the feeling of floating was God holding me in His hands as I was falling apart. He was with me; I just didn't realize it. That was the first time I would experience the touch of God personally, being held, but it would not be the last.

Once I told Randy my news, he went to get his results, and he was negative. I could not believe it. How could he be negative? I knew all about his life, and I thought that he for sure should be if I was. I was judging him because of his life.

Randy was good about it all. He tried to reassure me that it would all be ok. We had lots of people we knew with H.I.V. A friend of ours was on the board of the National Institute of Health (NIH). He was a member of a presidential task force and had a hot line to the white house AIDS czar.

He kept telling me I was going to be just fine, but I could not get over the fact that it was me and not him who was infected. Why me? I had been going along all this time with a false sense of security. I chose to believe it could not happen to me, that I was special, and that there was no way I could get it. I was a fool living in a fool's paradise. Fort Lauderdale was, and is, a fantasy land, one that is based on sex and fueled by money with drugs as the acceptable, if not most desired, lifestyle. I got caught in my own trap.

Once back in Fort Lauderdale, I began to explore the club scene again. My life would consist of going to work, coming home, going out, drinking, the occasional sexual encounter, and repeat. That was not all I was hungry for. The more I partied, the more I wanted. Before long, I was out at the dance clubs doing drugs again, and I discovered online sex websites that would provide opportunities to search out both sex and drugs.

This began to include methamphetamines. I was addicted easily, and it wasn't long before I was snorting at my desk in order to get through the day. I would be so tired from being up for two to three days that I would need the added bump of crystal to get me through the day.

I started to self-isolate in my office. I quit going to lunch with Billy. I had a perpetual cold, so I would take naps for lunch at my desk. To anyone else it would have been a real concern, but not to Billy. He just allowed it because he was too messed up to see how messed up

I had become.

Before long, I was smoking meth in my office or in my truck in the parking lot. I needed the jolt that it gave me to get through eight hours of work. To be honest, I was late a lot. I probably was only there six hours instead of eight most days, but I was able to get away with it. Things would get worse, and it would all implode. I would lose my job, Billy would later retire, and he and his wife would both die of alcoholism within the decade.

Through all of this, my mother and sister tried to keep in daily contact with me. My mother could always tell when something was wrong with me. I have never been a good liar. I could never play poker because I would give my hand away.

Stacie, on the other hand, was easier to fool. She was consumed with finding justice for my brother. Her conversations with me were fraternal, not maternal. She was my friend, and I thought I could get away with more when talking to her.

She finally seemed to accept me, and there was no more distance between us. She watched *Ellen*, she had become more hip and perhaps more jaded by life, and she was going through her own crisis at home. We just didn't know it at the time.

Her talks with me may have seemed easier since I was so far away. My life didn't impact her daily, but for my mom I became the center of her life in many ways. My mom could tell something bad was going on. She just didn't know exactly what it was.

About this time, I went down the rabbit hole, and it would take me to places I would have never imagined. I would do certain things, and my life would become one I could not imagine. The thing about being deceived is you don't realize at the time how deceived you are. I thought I was just having fun. I was doing what I wanted, and I wasn't hurting anyone. It was just me and the people I partied with, that is the lie an addict believes.

I was addicted to both sex and drugs. My addiction to sex had begun in my pre-teens with masturbation, and now that I was in my forties, I was fully addicted to drugs as well. The first time I shot up was the beginning of a decade long struggle with I.V. drug use.

I had met someone online, and we agreed to meet at his friend's house. Even though I had never tried it, I said yes. It became a fire that was lit in me that would take years to put out. I was hooked.

For the next six months, I would spend all my time with this man. He was a drug dealer, but not a very good one. He was always broke, and he did more drugs than he sold. He lost his apartment, and I would be the hero to try and help out. That's one of my biggest flaws. I give too much without thinking. Within a year, I would see and do more things than I care to share with you at this time.

My life was a complete freak show. I was involved in so many things that embarrass me to this day. I had no conscience because I had completely drowned it out. Eventually, all the drugs and partying caught up with me. I was shooting up every couple of days, and under really bad conditions.

I developed a very bad staph infection. MRSA is what they called it, but my general practitioner didn't treat it right. He was an angry gay doctor who blamed the fact that he had H.I.V. on his partner cheating on him and doing drugs. So, my I.V. drug use just made him mad; in fact, his treatment of me may have made things worse.

After three weeks, I was admitted to the hospital near death. I had an infection of the blood that had started as a big abscess on one leg and had spread across my body, running from one leg over to the other. I was slowly dying. Even through the weeks of pain I was going through, I still did drugs.

I spent a week in the hospital and then three weeks at home on I.V. antibiotics. I had a port to my heart to kill the bacteria in my blood. That is how seriously I had damaged myself, but I just laughed it off. It was cool to my druggie buddies that I had a port. They wanted to know if I wanted to shoot up right into it.

It's hard to write this, thinking of how badly damaged my mind and body were at the time. The thrill and excitement of getting high was just a lie that I kept telling myself, and that the enemy, Satan, kept whispering in my ear. I knew deep within my soul what damage it did, and the lies it told. Drugs are an evil mistress that lies to you and tells you that this time will be different.

At work, I was able to somehow pull it all off as just a bad infection I had gotten. They knew nothing of the drug use, or if they suspected anything, they never let on. My friend Eileen and her team arranged for me to work remotely from home once I was released from the hospital. I would still be homebound during the recovery period of two-to-three months before I would be well enough to go back to full time work in West Palm.

These people cared for me and tried to give me every chance to keep my job, but the addiction was stronger than the desire to keep my job. Before long, I was well enough to party again. I just wouldn't do as much this time. I told myself that I would be more careful, but I still had the drug dealer B.F. in my life.

It wasn't long before I found myself kicked out of my apartment. I had lost my job, but I had insurance money from the lost wages. I was able to convince myself that I could make it again.

Things didn't improve. I maintained the same crazy lifestyle of sex and drugs, and it was all that my life consisted of. I don't know what happened exactly for my family to figure out how bad things had become, but I probably had one of my famous conversations with my mother that freaked her out. I was most likely incoherent and making no sense.

If mom could not reach me on the phone, she would then text. If I avoided the text, she would call and call and plead with me to call her back. If I responded to the text, my responses would not make sense. She would ask a question, and it would take a day for me to reply. This was not the relationship we had built back, and I was now causing her to fear for my life on a daily basis.

I remember the day I got a knock on the door from the Fort Lauderdale Police Department. I was scared to death. I knew I had drugs in the house, and I was afraid they had finally come for me. It had only been about three months since the drug dealer B.F. got busted. However, they had just come to do a well check on me. My father had called and wanted them to let me know he loved me and wanted me to call him.

CHAPTER XIV

REHAB #1

My first bottom came in 2004, when I called my sister and told her I needed help. She arranged for me to get into La Hacienda. It was one of the best Drug and Alcohol Rehabs in the United States located in Hunt, Texas. It was a long plane ride back to Texas, and I was absolutely out of my mind when I arrived at the airport.

I had decided to sell as many of my possessions as I could and go have one big blow out of sex and drugs before I went to rehab. This is not a sane thing anyone does! It's not logical to say, "Hey! I have a problem, and since I have a problem, let's go celebrate it and have a big, final party!"

This, sadly, is how many people actually end up dead before rehab, but God was there all along. He didn't give up on me.

On the flight to Texas, I spent an hour in the toilet sketched-out, looking for drugs in the walls of the plane. I was one messed up dude, and it must have been evident to everyone but me. I don't know how I didn't get arrested. This was after September 11, and there were almost always sky marshals on the flights in and out of Fort Lauderdale. But I was spared again.

When I got to Texas, my parents picked me up, and we headed to my sister's in College Station. That is when they broke the news to me that the only way I could get into rehab was to be admitted to a Psychiatric Hospital first, and then be transferred to rehab.

I was devastated. I felt like I had been played. It would be a long time before I would trust my family again, but they were doing this for my own good. I was sick. Anyone who saw me could tell; anyone else would say I was a dead man walking.

Checking oneself into the "nut house" isn't fun. I could not understand why I had to be there. It was a seventy-two hour hold for a doctor to evaluate me so that he could tell me that I hated my father, that I was abused, etc. Most everything this shrink had to say was so far off course. Even in my state of mind, I could tell he had no idea how to help anyone. He was a textbook guy who just put a label on it and threw some pills at it.

Thankfully, the three days ended, and I was able to go to rehab. It's funny writing this now, how it took three days, like Jesus' death and resurrection, I had to die a little in order to be rehabilitated. The question was how much I was willing to die?

After I was released from the nut house, I went to the funny farm. LOL! That is what I call rehab. They kept telling me I was sick, and I would never be cured, but if I would only do these twelve steps for the rest of my life, I might make it. If I failed, I could repeat it over and over and over.

It didn't make any sense to me, but whatever I had to do to get fixed and get out of there! That was my real mentality. I didn't want to change inside. I just wanted to take a break, put things back together and move on. I had been placed in a counseling group led by a lady that probably had as many problems as I did. She did not seem to have ever conquered them. She just kept placing new band-aids on them. It was written all over her face, but she was sweet and reminded me of my grandmother when she spoke. Her soft reassuring voice led me to believe I would be fine if I just didn't do drugs, went to meetings, and worked the steps.

Steps, Step, Steps…. Well, I didn't go to meetings when I got out. That wasn't for me. I was smarter than these folks. I could see the flaw in the plan they were selling. They had taken God out of the equation and inserted another "higher power". I may have been a very backslidden Christian, but I knew that without God, this wasn't going to work for me. It wasn't going to cure anyone, failure was assured, and relapse was to be expected.

There was no shame in relapse, and there should not be any, but trying to do everything in your own strength won't work. Most of the people I met were alcoholics. I thought, "Well, I'm not an alcoholic. I just like to do drugs, and now that I've quit, I'm fixed!"

I blamed everyone else for my problems: my parents, my ex-wife, and my ex-boyfriends; everyone but me! I was a ticking time bomb!

My parents came to see me on the weekends, and we would have good visits. I used all the new techniques my counselors had taught me about setting boundaries with my parents. Basically, I became a bit of a bully to my dad. I was angry with him. I don't think I even knew what I was angry about, but it came out.

It must have been very hard to have your child, that you love, try and put you in your place. I am so ashamed of the way I treated my father. My dad is an honorable man that has done nothing but try to live for the Lord his whole life. When he tried to have input into my adult life, I balked at it. I made boundaries with him.

In hindsight, I can see that I was doing to him what I had done to God. I had put God in a box and was doing the same to my parents.

There were lines that I didn't want them to cross. I was insisting on having things my way. When you put it into those words, it kind of sounds like a three-year-old having a tantrum, and in many ways I was. What I didn't see, what I couldn't see because I was so blind to my own self will, is that my parents were just trying to help me. They loved me. When they would ask questions, I would flare up in my feelings and declare them invalid.

I was expressing the culture in my life. If you wanted a relationship with me, it had to be on my terms. How very selfish I was, but my parents held it together most of the time. They had all their friends praying for me. I got cards, calls, and letters from my parents' friends. I also had my core gay friends that expressed concern, love, and anger.

You can always tell what kind of relationship you have with your friends or family by the way someone loves you. Pure love, God's love, covers a multitude of sins and hurts, but any other form of love will not. That is when you see the angry side from people that claim to love you.

True love for one another shares in the pain someone is going through, whereas any other form of love sets boundaries. Cross that boundary, and I may not love you anymore. You might not get invited on the next trip. You may get punished for being human.

From my vantage point now, I see that "cancel culture" is destroying our society. It is Godless, and those who do it expect everyone else to bow down to their feelings. This is why I think Christ has been canceled, even by many Christians. They don't want to hear what He is saying. They don't want anyone to have input into their lives.

I certainly didn't want my parents' input, but I would take their money… the $2,500.00 it took to get into rehab in 2004.

Twenty-eight days later ... That's how long rehab usually lasts because that's how long insurance is willing to pay for it. After that, it's up to you to do the work. Upon completion of my staycation in 2004, I was awarded with a little bronze key chain medallion. It read, "To thine own self be true." You see, everyone gets a participation trophy in rehab.

I left feeling great and in charge. My family wanted me to stay in Texas, but I was dead set against it. I wanted to get back to Florida as fast as I could. I had my things and my friends and the beach. I wanted life on my terms and to be as far away from my family as I could be.

I just wanted to participate in the family, but not be invested in it. Phone calls, the occasional holiday, but nothing deep and meaningful, if it had to do with my parents. I blamed them for so much that had gone wrong in my life. I failed to take into account my role in anything. As far as I was concerned, I was just some poor innocent bystander in my life that was being beat up.

My feelings got hurt. I was acting like a child. I wanted my way, and I was horrible if I didn't get it. Of course, I could always try to manipulate my folks, or at least I thought I could. The funny thing about how you see yourself, and the way others see you, is it's not always the same. If you find a group of people that validate all your feelings, beware, it's usually a trap!

After I returned to Florida, I quickly got a new job. My employer in West Palm had terminated me. They had no choice, but the insurance had paid for thirty-thousand dollars' worth of rehab. My boss, Eileen, must have pulled some strings for me. I cannot to this day figure out how all that worked out, but fortunately, it did. Between Eileen and my family, I was able to get through this latest episode of "The life and times of *Steve, Alive* once again".

The new job had no idea of my drug history. They had only known that I had been seeking medical treatment, and with HIV, it was easy to claim a disability. It wasn't long until I would be walking down the same road I had been down and trying to pull myself up by myself. It would cost me that job and a few others, but I kept getting clean and relapsing.

They say the definition of insanity is doing the same thing over and over and expecting a different result. That is the addict mentality. Not seeking healing and restoration, but reprieve, forgiveness, and along with that, permission to do it all over again.

You see, allowing yourself to believe you are a victim of your disease, genetics, or your past gives you permission to fail over and over again. It is why I have such a problem with twelve-step programs. As long as God has no power, then you're only able to stay sober on your own if you have enough support to hold your fragile little ego together.

Don't get me wrong. Twelve-step programs help a lot of people, but they usually stop at the higher power and let you figure it out on your own and fail on your own.

Jesus, on the other hand, never gives up on you. He is not just a *higher power*. He is THE ONLY POWER that can overcome all the pain, guilt, trauma, shame, regret, anger, hurt, and abuse that a life of sin can bring. Addicts are just sinners in need of salvation, and that is something that AA and twelve-step programs have a hard time with. They want to give you a step up and a road to power but won't tell you who it is or show you the path to that power. It's false flags!

CHAPTER XV

SECOND CHANCES

My life after Rehab in 2004 was a series of ups and downs on my own. I could not fight the desire to do drugs. I was doing it all on my own, no Jesus. I had become my own "Higher Power" and I was failing at it.

I would have periods of weeks and months without any drug use, but all of my other old habits remained the same. I didn't realize it at the time, but God wanted all of me to change. He wanted complete control, and I was a control freak in every way. This much and no more of me.

I believed in Jesus and the Bible, but not everything; only what I wanted to believe. This piece-meal mentality will only get you mixed results, and that's exactly what happened to me. My relationship with the Lord had become a check-in-check-out religion, without any close relationship with the Father.

I eventually got a steady job at a terrible title company that had no integrity. I could tell it from the mafia guys that ran the closings, to the owner that would sell her soul for a good premium if we would agree to look the other way on title issues.

This put a bad taste in my mouth. I personally cannot stand to see lack of integrity. That's funny, considering how little I had myself.

I looked for new jobs constantly, but I could not find a better job than the one I had. I had a guy that was my supervisor that had less than two years of experience in the industry telling me that I was to do things his way, which were usually wrong and ended up having to be redone again later because of his need to be in control and wield power over a group of underlings.

During this time, I actually spent quite a bit of time in prayer. I would ask God why he still had me at this job that I hated when good jobs were always available…just not to me. I heard him say, "I'm teaching you patience."

And that is exactly what He was doing. I have always been impatient. It's probably my worst personality flaw, and it's the one that he wanted to start working on first. I did not understand it at first, but soon it would all make sense.

I had been dating a guy from my hometown of Midland, Texas, that I met in Fort Lauderdale. Dave was a nice guy, very kind and intelligent. He was just as broken as I was, and yet I was always trying to fix him. I played pastor, healer, and counselor to his victim mentality.

Dave and I had been talking about leaving Florida and heading back to Texas. The real estate market was at an all-time high, and it was a perfect time for Dave to cash out and sell his house. We would move to Dallas, but poor Dave and his victim mentality made it impossible for him to make rational decisions, especially after spending half the night drinking enough booze to drown a sailor. We were two broken people trying to help each other. Dave would drink to drown out the pain he held inside, and I would get to a point I couldn't help him and bail on him. I would go and get high and disappear for a day or two.

That crazy up and down lifestyle was driving us apart, and soon, I would have my exit. In August of 2005, Hurricane Katrina started a downward decline in the housing market in Fort Lauderdale, and by October of 2005 with Hurricane Wilma the housing market and the economy of south Florida was dead. I had been trying to get Dave to sell the house for six months, but he wanted to wait, hoping the market would only get higher. He was wrong. It tanked overnight and so did his job, and mine as well.

I decided to leave and head home to Texas. God had given me an exit. That first lesson in patience God was teaching me had meant that when I got laid off, I had two-hundred five dollars a week of unemployment benefits from the State of Florida to move away on.

It wasn't much, but it covered my car payment, my cell phone bill, and my insurance. My folks helped with the rest until I was on my feet.

I was excited to leave Florida! I drove from Fort Lauderdale to Mobile, Alabama on the first day. Seeing the destruction along the coast of the Southeast of the United States was absolutely the most destruction I had ever seen in my life. It looked like a war zone in many areas. New Orleans was disgusting with its underpasses layered with cars and covered in 4 feet of damp mud that smelled of decay and death. I could not get out of Louisiana quick enough.

When I finally made it to my sister's house in College Station, I felt like I had a huge weight lifted off my shoulders. Florida was no longer part of my life other than friends, and those relationships would not last either.

Things in Texas started off well enough. I had family and old friends in Texas. I could make a fresh start, and that was what I intended to do. The only problem with making a fresh start is you can never really do that as long as you bring your old baggage with you.

Things seemed to begin to fall into place, and I was soon back in Midland doing the job I had been trained to do working in Oil and Gas. I was making great money. Everything looked rosy on paper, but I can mess anything up on my own, and I tried my best to do just that.

It wasn't long before I was seeking out men that had a similar drug history as me. The hookup websites had codewords that let you know what kind of "fun" someone was into, and I knew all the lingo. I was always on the lookout for guys that liked to PNP, that's the code for Party and Play with drugs. These sites were nothing more than glorified sex sites. They called them dating sites, but that is not what goes on in reality.

I opened up the box and decided to spin the wheel once more. The funny thing is that when I was doing it, I knew it was wrong. I would rationalize at the time that the only thing wrong was the drugs, that the sex was just something that everyone does, and that I wasn't hurting anyone. But I was always hurting someone. I was always hurting myself to begin with, then there were the people that depended on my services for work; there was my family and friends, and the one I always forgot about was Jesus and the Holy Spirit that lived within me.

I think for many years I rationalized this on some level. Kind of like, God doesn't have to know about this, or I wasn't that bad, or lots of people do bad things.

That kind of rationalization of behavior will allow your mind to try and convince your heart that you're not as bad as you really are. The truth of the matter was that my life was nearing a crossroads, and I didn't know it. I had not yet made it to the intersection, but it was up ahead.

Once I hit the dead end it would require a decision. The odd thing about going down a dead-end road is there are always lots of clues that it's a dead-end road. For me, and I'm sure millions of other people, we have lived our lives not looking at the signs along the road.

In the midst of all of this, I was trying to figure out how to reconnect with my children. It's hard to imagine why they would have wanted to know me after what they went through, but in my mind, I was always the victim. The one thing I am most certain of in life is that when you truly love someone, nothing can ever fully break that bond. It can be strained to the point of putting distance between one another, but the longing to be together never ends.

It never ended with me towards my kids. That longing was part of the heartache that I tried to drown out with drugs, sex, expensive cars, jewelry, art, and anything that would give me a momentary sense of calm or numbness to my feelings. I didn't realize I was doing it at the time, but it was perfectly clear to someone with twenty-twenty vision what was going on in my life behind the scenes in my mind.

The struggle of life as a gay man was one of expectation, disappointments, judgment, and shame. I struggled with these feelings constantly. I was able to conceal it pretty well, but when I had too much, I would go back to drugs again. I just didn't seem to know how to live on my own.

During this time, the relationship with my family deepened. I began to allow them back into my life a little at a time, and the more I let them in the more things seemed to get better. One day, my father informed me that my sons were working at a local tire store, and that I might try and see if I could find them and reach out to them.

According to my divorce attorney, my termination of my parental rights included a permanent restraining order. The boys were both over eighteen, and any restraining order I was under to stay away from them was no longer valid; however, it was still in place for my daughter. I knew that the only way to get back any relationship with them was through the boys.

They both had known me long enough to know me as their father. That bond was still there, I was certain of it. It took me several weeks to gain the courage to actually go to the tire store and inquire about them. I would drive by and look in the bays to see if I could see them.

My fear kept me from acting for a little while, but one day I drove by and saw my son Jaret changing tires. This was my moment if I was ever going to take it.

I went into the shop. When the salesman called me up to the counter and asked what he could do for me, I asked if that was Jaret, and he said yes. I gave the man my business card and asked him to give it to him. I said that Jaret would know who I was. That was it, I took a baby step towards regaining a relationship with my children. It wasn't any grand gesture or gift trying to make up for lost time, it was just my business card.

I left the tire store and went on with my life. Things were not in my control, and I knew it, but I had made an effort. That was the turning point for me in many ways. Life continued on, and weeks went by. I never got the phone call I expected.

Then one day in the fall of 2007, quite by chance, I was looking at my emails and there was an email from Jaret. It was a miracle! He had reached out. But it was not a friendly email, it was an angry email. Apparently, he had sent an email weeks earlier and it went to my spam folder. Satan was working hard to keep us apart.

In that email, he lashed out at me, "Why did you give me this card if you aren't going to respond to me?" There were several other angry outbursts. He was still a hurt little boy. He was grown, but inside the little boy was still hurting.

I quickly fired off several emails. I was begging for him to give me another chance. I pleaded with him not to push me away, and somehow, I broke through the wall of doubt he had. He didn't want to meet at first, he just wanted to talk on the phone. I was on cloud nine! I had a chance, and I was going to make sure this time I didn't mess it up. I don't remember what all was said on that first call, but I do remember that the ice broke quickly. He was still the sweet, kind young man that I had met at my brother's funeral.

We set a date to meet at my apartment. I would cook dinner for us, and we could talk about anything. The days leading up to that day were some of the most stressful and exciting days. I kept worrying that he might back out or that his mother would convince him not to come.

When the day came, he showed up on time. That day was one of the best days of my life! I have pictures from that day. I had a camera with a timer on a tripod set up so we could have our picture taken together. I had pulled out the fine china and crystal, and I set a banquet for my son. I had worked for days cleaning the house, making sure everything was just right.

When Jaret walked through my front door all the hurt of thirteen years started to fall away. We sat on the couch, and he wanted to hear my side of the story. Why I left, why I never came back, why I never called. He did not understand why I had abandoned them.

Telling him why was hard. Telling him all the things that had transpired between his mother, grandmother, and me and the issues with CPS, they were difficult conversations to have. I didn't want to make them out to be monsters, but at the same time I needed him to know that I made mistakes and that they had made a few as well.

It wasn't hard for him to understand that side of his grandmother. He had seen it in other family situations. I reminded him of the newspaper across the windshield incident. He had never forgotten that day either. The hurt that his mother caused that day was still with him thirteen years later.

Tracy and I had done a lousy job of protecting our children because we did not work as a unit. We had no plan for our lives, and when things fell apart between us the reactions were to go to our corners fighting instead of finding any common ground.

I don't know what would have happened to us if we had decided to try and work things out. Maybe God would have worked things out in my life sooner than later, but that is not what happened. The divide was too deep, and the die had been cast - we would be enemies.

That adversarial relationship did not end with Tracy once our divorce was over. She was not going to admit to any fault. She had dug her feet in and denied me any relationship with my children.

The hurt that she felt must have been devastating to her. I can only imagine what that kind of pain feels like, to see your world crumble and to have to admit your husband left you for another man. That is a pain that is covered in shame. That pain will build walls that are impenetrable.

However, for Jaret and me, our relationship started off great. The pictures from those early days are ones with big wide grins on our faces. We were a family again even if it was just us two. I had tried reaching out to both Jason and Jade but was informed that Jason wanted nothing to do with me. Jade, on the other hand, had her mom, stepfather, and her grandparents persuading her to not let me in.

Jade and I eventually became friends on Myspace. That seemed like an opening, but very soon, it would close. I have always been an emotional person, and I made several mistakes in my early days of social media. I would see a post and instantly think it had something to do with me. How self-centered of me to think that every time a teenage girl posts something on social media that it is all about the person that is reading it.

It's very bizarre, in reality, to think that a post that does not name you and isn't sent to you personally is somehow all about you because you read yourself into the situation. That is what an insecure person will do anytime they are feeling threatened.

I also have been known to lack a filter when speaking. I give advice too freely, and think I have the answers to many things that I have not been asked to solve. I am a helper by nature. I love other people, and that love for other people often leads me to sticking my neck on the line for someone that is not looking for my support, or able to receive support without feeling threatened.

I tend to create many more problems in my life because I act impulsively. It is always with plenty of good intentions, but those good intentions are not usually what God has planned for my life or the life of the other people or situation that I am pushing my way into. Learning to wait on God, letting Him direct my path, and not getting in front of Him, is a lesson that I expect to be learning for the rest of my life.

God's timing is His not ours. He knows just what we need. If someone like me keeps pushing into areas that we are not intended to be in, we do not help God or the people we are trying to help. We become stumbling blocks for them and get ourselves way off course with God's plan.

Luckily for me, my timing and my decision to follow the Spirit and reach out to Jaret had produced fruit. We had begun a new relationship. He had cousins and family he had never met, and grandparents that were overjoyed to have him in their lives again.

Things were beginning to look up for me, and I was excited about my future. I was drug free at the time. I was staying on the right road. Though my relationship with Jesus was still very one-sided it seemed, little by little, I was beginning to develop a new relationship with Him.

Around this time, I started to attend a Gay Evangelical Church in Midland. I know that sounds like an oxymoron, but gays that were raised as Christians still have the same desire to commune with God and one another. Many times, these congregations are places where wounded people that have found God and stopped drinking and drugging come together to find like-minded people to worship together.

In many ways, it is not any different from any other Protestant church that has a set of beliefs that they go by. If you go to a Presbyterian or Methodist Church, they have certain beliefs that describe who they are as congregations. In the gay churches, it is usually that God loves everyone, and that he never makes a mistake, so you are perfect just the way you are.

I would call it "*Pentecostal light*", but the difference between a true Pentecostal church and a gay church is that sin is always sin in a Pentecostal church. In a gay church, the sin of homosexuality is a lifestyle choice and not relevant.

The funny thing is that the Holy Spirit still showed up in that gay church. For years, I tried to understand how it could be possible that the theology could be so counter to the gospel, but the spirit still moved there. Finally, it hit me. The Bible says that when two or more are gathered in My name, I am there. He was in those of us that were saved.

We were still sinners like everyone else, and our sin had not completely separated us from Him. It may have deeply hurt Him, but it did not separate us. He already died for all our sins, the ones in the past and the ones in the future. He knows everything about us, and he loves us with a love that passes all understanding. He is grace, He is mercy, and He is the definition of love.

I now had a new purpose in life. A new lease on it, as it were. With my son Jaret back in my life, I began to experience true joy again for the first time in decades. I was a happy man, and I saw such a bright future ahead of me and Jaret. My disappointment in not having a relationship with Jason and Jade did not disappear just by having Jaret back in my life, but the fact that he was back gave me hope for more to come.

It does not matter how often you are told "No", if you really want something, that longing for what you are searching for never completely goes away. With Jaret back, I was able to breathe again and not be so angry at life and God, and I began to forgive Tracy for some of the grievances I had against her.

That little light that Jaret brought back into my life was melting away hurts and allowing me to see how I had been at fault. This wonderful new world was about to be rocked. I had no idea at the time how much I would lose when it was all said and done.

By the spring of 2007, I had taken a position at a small oil and gas company in Sweetwater, Texas. The company was full of misfits. I think most people would have just said "No" to the job, but I was on a path to making a name for myself. I finally had established myself professionally again in Texas, and I wanted great things. I had a desire for wealth and wanted to take a leap, and grasp for the gold ring.

Unfortunately, the only gold was in the name of the company. All other wealth was being drained out of the company as fast as it could come in. The vultures had descended upon this company by invitation, bad choices, and lack of vision. Greed and lust for success had taken control of the owners, and I became a pawn in a game of whack-a-mole on a corporate level.

During that same time, while I was chasing my dreams, Jaret decided he wanted to follow in my footsteps and become a landman, too. I was quite pleased as any father would be that his son wanted to follow in his footsteps. I guided him towards the only company that I knew that had a training program for young men wanting to learn the trade, that might be willing to give him a chance, and he got the job. Jaret had the same natural intuition for the job as I had. He picked it up quickly, and I was very proud of him.

Meanwhile, I was beginning to see my personal life take new directions. Someone I had been dating exited my life, and a new person entered it. I was on a never-ending search for 'Mister Right'. I had no idea what that meant, I just kept looking.

During this new season of life, things in my relationship with Jaret began to have its first, real bumps in the road. Jaret had come to my home for a family holiday. During that visit, I was showing my mother around the house. She always liked to look at the many things I collected. There was a small inlaid silver box that I had purchased years before that was lying on a coffee table. My mother asked me what was in it, and I said it had a pain pill and Xanax in it.

She opened it, and it was empty. I knew that I had just filled it the day before, and that I didn't take any of the pills. That was just in case I needed to take a pill box on the road. Of course, I knew that the only person that had been at the house all the time was my son. My young nieces and nephew had not seen it, and my mom asked Jaret if he had seen the pills.

He got very irritated at the question; his guilt was showing all over him. The old saying, "I think thou dost protest too much," is true. I was disappointed, and he decided to leave early. I guess he could not stand the heat. My mother is relentless at times, and she kept asking questions and prying. That made him very uncomfortable.

It made me very sad that I could not trust my son. This caused a noticeable change in our relationship. It wasn't long before we would all have to face the fact that Jaret had a drug problem. After one weekend trip to see me, he left early, and said he was headed to a friend at Possum Kingdom Lake. I was disappointed he was leaving, but he was grown and could make his own decisions.

On Monday morning following that weekend, I got a voicemail from my ex-wife, Tracy. I could tell by the tone of the voice in the voicemail that I was somehow in trouble. I didn't know what for, but her voice was heavy with accusations and demanded that I call her.

I don't know what actually transpired with Jaret that weekend. It is not something we ever discussed. All I know is he came home to his mother's, and he was acting weird. He was obviously on drugs, and because he had been at my place, I was under suspicion.

The truth is I didn't realize he had a problem. I had never asked, and he had never told me anything. Tracy and I had no communication, so I had no idea what was going on in his life, other than what little he shared with me. I was blindsided by the phone call when Tracy and I spoke. Somehow, what was wrong with Jaret was my fault, and once again Tracy wanted me out of the picture. I offered my help. I even shared my experience of rehab with her and told her I would help, but that help was not wanted or accepted. In her mind, I was the cause of all the problems, and I was asked to stay out of things. She and Ross would take care of it.

The saddest thing about all this was Tracy had attributed Jaret's drug problems to me - like father, like son. The truth of the matter is there was some truth to this, I'm sure, but I had not been in his life to shape it, good or bad. So, I wasn't sure why I was being blamed for a problem that she had been dealing with for quite some time before I came back into the picture. I was lost and guilty, and I was scared for my son.

Fortunately, Jaret had health insurance and could get treatment. At least that was the thinking. I tried to give some input, but it was rejected. Tracy and Ross had made a plan, one that was rubber stamped by some foolish doctor that claimed that a week of outpatient treatment would cure him, and that he did not have a real drug problem.

I don't know how much of this had to do with the fact that Ross was running for public office at the time, and they wanted to get this swept under the rug; how much was naivety, or just how good a B.S.-er Jaret was, but regardless, Jaret was declared cured in a week. That is the fastest I've ever known of any drug treatment plan in the history of addiction. One band-aid and you're cured.

If only it was that easy. I know a lot about addiction, and the one thing I know is that the damage that is done to the brain takes years to repair. I also know that the only physician that could ever cure you on the spot was Jesus. Even though I know there were people praying for Jaret to get well, the fact that not many people even knew he had a problem made it difficult for the body of Christ to act as a body and come together and pray as a body for Jaret's needs.

CHAPTER XVI

THE VALLEY OF DEATH

In January of 2010, I was preparing to move back to Midland. An old family friend had hired me to manage her land title brokerage firm. Preparations were under way for a move. One Sunday afternoon, I received a call from Jaret. He had been thrown out of his home by his mother and stepfather. It was late January, the weather had been very cold into the twenties, and he was living in his truck.

This time he admitted the truth to me. He had used drugs. He told me about the problem, and what had transpired at home. For the first time, Jaret confided in me about his problems. He opened up to me and became vulnerable. He needed his daddy. I told him to head to a local motel; that I would have a room waiting for him when he arrived; to take a hot shower, put on some warm clothes, and that I would be in Midland as quickly as I could. We would figure things out.

I know I was in shock, but I was a little happy with the fact that he had reached out to me. That might sound odd, but for the first time in nearly two decades I was able to meet a need he had, and he reached out to me. I know how I felt. All the fatherly instincts came back naturally; I had a child to rescue. I can only imagine how our Father in heaven must feel each time we go astray and then come back to him.

That genuine joy in my son for choosing to call me was one of pure affection and pride. I was proud to be called daddy, and I was proud to be wanted. I know that is hard to say, but it's true. I wanted to be wanted. I wanted to be needed. I wanted to be the one to save the day.

There! I said it! That little bit of pride was not of God. That is not the way the Father sees his children when He rescues them from the clutches of evil. I was wrong to feel any pride in being the "savior". I am not a savior, and I am not capable of saving anyone. I have tried many times and failed at all the attempts I've made. The only person I can possibly save is myself, by giving myself over to the Holy Spirit and letting him guide me.

I found an extended stay hotel for us to live in until I was able to acquire an apartment for us. It would not be just Jaret and me; it would also be my boyfriend Zach, his two cats, and my two dogs. The seven of us would need a big apartment. I was fortunate to find one that was very large. It was perfect for such an experiment with one bedroom, two baths, three living rooms, a dining room, and a kitchen on the main floor. It also had two bedrooms and baths on the second floor.

I went into full designer mode and purchased furniture to outfit Jaret a bedroom. I spoiled him. I was doing everything I could to try and make him happy. He was able to have his girlfriend over, and I didn't object to the two of them sleeping together. How could I? I was living in sin with my boyfriend.

I was able to get Jaret a job working with me as a landman. He was on cloud nine it seemed. We worked very well together. I was amazed at how well we worked together and at how smart he was. He was able to do everything just like me. His skills were spot on when it came to intuitiveness with running title.

I have to say I felt some pride there too; I think it was good pride. I was proud to have a son that was "a chip off the old block", as they say. That very same pride would eat my lunch later on. Living together as a little family, the three of us with the dogs and cats was normal. It seemed normal, but I recall that one day he overheard the bickering between Zach and me. His response to it caught me off guard. He said, "Y'all sound like Meemaw and Daddy Weldon"… Tracy's folks.

This really did not sit well with me. I did not like these people, and the feelings were mutual I'm certain. Being compared to someone you do not like is a very humbling experience, and one that I hope I don't ever have to go through again. The key to that is to forgive and love people as they are.

I am trying my best to live that out today. I admit it's not always easy, but it is my goal to live as Christ instructed us: to love one another as ourselves. Proverbs 16:18 (NAS) says,

> *"Pride goes before destruction, and a haughty spirit before stumbling."*

I didn't know it then, but I would most certainly fall and stumble because of my pride. The fall would be devastating in its destruction of strongholds in my life. This is the blessing of the fall: it provides the opportunity to rebuild on solid ground.

Of course, the most important thing in my mind was my relationship with Jaret. I wanted him to get clean and stay clean, but it's hard to set a good example when you are not living it yourself. You see, the apple didn't fall far from the tree. I had a drug problem too. Only mine was legal, so I didn't think mine was a problem. I was under doctors' orders.

I had prescriptions for Hydrocodone, and lots of it. As someone with a bad back, I was prescribed thousands of Hydrocodone in between the years of 2005 and 2018. I was hooked on them, but I was able to dole out only what I needed on a daily basis.

I kept my stash in a hiding place because of Jaret. I thought I was so smart, but it turned out that my son was very much like me in many ways. As I said before, my grandmother used to say if you ever want to know where something is, ask Steve. He's nosey, and he will know where it is. It turns out that Jaret was nosey, too. He had found my stash. I had hidden the pills in a boot in my closet, and I had forgotten even where they were because I was not using as many at the time.

I had hidden a new bottle with one hundred pills in the boot, and when I pulled the bottle out it was nearly empty with only thirty pills left. Seventy pills were missing. It didn't take a genius to figure out what happened to them. I was hurt, sad, and angry, but I kept my cool.

Instead of roaring and throwing a fit about it, I decided to get rid of the pills and put a note in the bottle, which I left in the boot. The note read, "Jaret, I think we need to talk. You have a problem. Dad".

I didn't know how long he had been getting into the pill bottle, but I knew he would come back to it. That is what addicts do when they know the drug of choice is available. It didn't take long for Jaret to find the note. When he came to me, we had a long talk. I explained to him how scared I was and that I didn't want to lose him. I was afraid of what would happen to him, and I didn't want to have to tell his mother he was dead.

We had a nice long cry and hugged. I told him that I had hired a family friend, Anna, who was a substance abuse counselor, to come and help him. They would meet each week and I would pay for the first several sessions. Then, he would start paying for them. I thought I made a good decision to hire an addiction specialist for Jaret. I didn't think that I had any problem that needed to be dealt with, but I made a stupid decision to make him start paying for them instead of paying for them myself.

On the outside, things looked ok, but I knew he was still struggling. I confronted him a couple of times, but he always denied it. The funny thing is that all the signs of his using drugs were right in front of my face; however, Jaret was a good liar, and he could put on a good show. Even with the constant money problems and the inability to pay his bills while living for free and being paid very well, I could not see the forest for the trees. I saw a son I loved and was so happy to have him in my home that I overlooked the problems until I could not overlook them anymore.

When Jaret decided to cut back his counseling sessions to once every two weeks instead of once a week I should have known better and objected, but I did not object. I kept my mouth closed and let him make his own decision. That is a decision I deeply regret. If I had not been so blind to everything going on I might have seen that this was a plea for help.

On the morning of May 12, 2010, I woke up like any other morning. I was getting ready for work and was about to head out the door to the office when I noticed that Jaret's alarm clock was going off in his room. I called to him several times, but he did not answer.

When I opened the door, I saw him lying there curled up in the fetal position. I called to him. I tried to wake him, but he was gone. I knew when I saw him that he was dead. The details of the nine-one-one call and the attempts at C.P.R. were useless. He had passed hours earlier, around four a.m.

I had to make all the calls one never wants to make in these circumstances. I was beside myself in shock and grief. My boyfriend came home. He was the one that stepped in and called my family for me. I don't recall too much else other than friends started showing up to be with me. It wouldn't be long before Tracy, all her family, and our children, Jason, and Jade, would show up. The chaos of death brought us together if only for a moment.

I remember that in one moment Jason was hurting badly and I went to comfort him. He hugged me and I told him how much his brother had loved him, and that I loved him, too. For one brief moment I got to hold my other son again. In his pain I was his daddy once more for a moment.

For one brief moment it appeared that we would all be allowed to grieve together as a family. Ross invited me and my family to come to his home and that we could make plans there. Before I could get there, I got a call from Ross informing me that we had been uninvited. The funeral would be a lot like my divorce, with two opposing sides.

The shock that I felt with Jaret's death suddenly was lifted away. I had people that showed up and loved me. It was as if I was able to float throughout the process. Things that would cause my family to get upset in the natural world with the way Tracy and her family treated us, they did not affect me because of God's supernatural power. I chose to let them grieve and take myself out of the situation, personally, as to my feelings.

This was God's love surrounding me in a very real way. That floating that I felt was His hands holding me, cradling me in love. I could feel it, and it allowed me to make decisions without anger or resentment during that time. I was able to let his mother, brother, and sister deal with their grief without pushing myself on them.

As we went through the process of death, I saw love, and I gave of myself instead of demanding my own way. This was not easy. It was very difficult, but I was able to do it in this one instance. I chose to make myself last and not first. My feelings did not matter, being right didn't matter, being loved by the people I loved who despised me did not matter.

It hurt to know that these people despised me, but I was able to walk with grace and dignity throughout it. Not because I was walking alone, but because God was walking alongside me. He was holding my hand, and He already bore all the pain I was feeling by His Son, Jesus', death. Therefore, He was able to walk me through the process and allow me to give others the space they needed to grieve without making it the Steve Show.

The darkest days of my life gave me the strength to make choices that said you are not number one, and you do not need to be the center of things. A tiny voice was saying to me, "Let me handle this."

This was the way the Spirit dealt with it. He protected me and my feelings, and He allowed me to walk through the battlefield in those days. The fight was still ongoing; the storm of life had not passed. I was just not caught up in it at that moment; peace like a river attended my soul, and I was able to be at peace in the midst of great chaos and loss.

This feeling would not last, but it was the first time in my life I felt with all real certainty the love and power of God's presence. That love was, and still is, the only thing I have ever known for certain that is real in this world.

The pain of rejection was the very same pain that Jesus experienced on the cross. With it He died to it. He willingly embraced all the pain I ever felt in order that I might be able to have eternal life. His sacrifice was so great. The shame, dishonor, and pain were so great that He endured for our sins. He was blameless, but He chose to take the sin of the world upon Himself, to bear them on the cross and to die to sin so that we might live.

Most people think of love as a feeling, but love is action, not feeling.

We can feel love because there is always action associated with it. To just go throughout life based on our feelings, we would be lost. Love guides us through the valleys of life. It walks beside us in our darkest days, and it shows up for us with strength we do not possess in order to carry us to the other side of a battle when we are wounded and cannot make it on our own.

One of the things that was related to me after Jaret's death, during the time I just floated through, was about Anna, Jaret's counselor, when she arrived on the scene. She was holding my hand and comforting me, and in that moment, she experienced a love she had never seen before.

She saw gay men and women come and shower me with love. She began to have a new vision of gay people as just people. People who were capable of loving others just like the rest of the world. How profoundly they showed love to me in my hour of grief was eye opening and life changing for her. She had never before experienced the love of God that was covering me that day.

For the first time in her life, she had seen and tasted the full love of God being showered on me in that moment. As a Christian, she had never understood gay people and had no way of seeing them other than as sinners. At that moment, she saw them as instruments used by God to comfort me. In that moment, she saw them as meek, not weak.

For so many believers, it is easy to see the sin and not the sinner.

Seeing one's sin and defining that person by it is blasphemy in my opinion. If we do not see each and every person as God's creation, no matter how bad the sin is, we are saying He made a mistake, and that He is somehow wrong.

The truth of the matter is that the majority of gay people are the most loving and kindest people you will ever meet. I think this is due in part to the fact that they do love, that they are meek in spirit, but that meekness has been cast as weakness by the world.

Weakness has applied other labels to people. The gay label is one that is easy to apply to meekness in a world that sees anything that is not viewed as strong as weakness; when in fact, the meekness is a testament to the fact that love is in the heart of the one that is meek. One of the signs of life is love, without love there is no life.

One of the things I have noticed in review of my past attempts to let God into my life, is my choosing when and how much control to give to him. When I first came back from San Francisco in 1986, I was all in when I was left. But, by the time I had returned to Texas I started putting up roadblocks in my mind, saying, "This much and no more!" I have done this many times, and I realize how easy it is to do. When things get personal or too deep, "Whoa there! I am not sure I want to give you that much of me," is the reaction.

Like when I decided to marry Tracy, I was only willing to give so much of myself to the relationship. I had already planned a fire escape, like an exit ramp, in case I could not handle the fire of married life. I was a one foot in one foot out kind of guy, and that was how I lived both physically and spiritually. The old saying, "Don't fence me in," described me very well.

The funny thing is I fooled myself and others into thinking I was all in. Maybe for a moment at a time I was, but as soon as I could not handle a situation, I would bail. That formula for life did not serve me well, and it is not acceptable to Christ. He was always there with me.

Looking at my life, I am certain of His love and patience. It's overwhelming to realize how much I hurt Him; how much He suffered with me because every road I went down He was there. He saw it all, and the image is more disturbing than I want to recall. My life was spent in the seediest of places. I have done things that I cannot bring myself to repeat, but God knows it all, and he still loves me!

He never gave up on me because He purchased me with His son Jesus Christ's blood on Calvary. My sin is not too much for Christ because he already knew it before I did. He held me when I was breaking apart and kept showing me the door, so that I would choose to leave behind the hurts that I had carried along the way.

In the summer of 2017, I was in a very bad place. I had placed my life at risk again with drugs and the path was beyond scary. I came so close to so many death traps, but He somehow saved my life. I remember one such occasion, I was driving back to Midland from

Hobbs, NM. I had been working in New Mexico, and I had gotten really strung out. I was at a crossroad in my life quite literally.

I had stopped for gas at a gas station all by itself on a road that had traffic teaming with law enforcement. This was drug cartel country, and the gangs were bad there. I could have ended up dead just for the crazy things I was doing by hanging out with drug dealers. I was quite nervous and coming down from being high made me extra sketchy. I was a mess when suddenly a man appeared next to me. He was selling something, a kind of shiny ribbon or pencils, I don't recall which, for Christian drug counseling. He asked me if I knew Jesus.

I was scared at first. Who was this person and where did he come from? He just appeared. No car, no bike, he was just suddenly next to me at the pump. I've long thought that this was Christ making a plea to me. At the time, I was dismissive of this person and just wanted to get away, but I recall he asked me a second time if I was in need of help. He was shining a light on my soul.

It made me uncomfortable, but that road was the road that led me here to where I am now. As awful as it was, I would not change a thing if it meant I didn't have the relationship I have with the Lord now. Jesus is my friend. He is my comforter. He is my strength and my salvation. He is everything to me, and I am so very, very grateful for His love!

CHAPTER XVII

THE FIRST TIME I DIED!

I entered this world on Friday, August 21, 1964 at 12:03 A.M., according to the hospital card notating the moment of my birth. Moments before that I was pronounced dead. I had been set aside by Dr. Parks who delivered me. I did not breathe because the cord had been wrapped around my neck. There happened to be an old, black nurse in the delivery room that picked me up and gave me mouth to mouth until I took my first breath and was pronounced alive. My first kiss, the breath of life that entered my lungs, was from a person whose name I will never know.

I was a full-term baby that had been slowly starving to death in the womb. I weighed three pounds, two and one-half ounces and was twenty-one and one-half inches long. I was skin and bones for a full-term baby.

Those were the days of Jim Crow laws and segregation, and this skinny little white boy's life was saved by a beautiful, black soul I have never met. I am certain that I am not the only baby she saved that way. This nurse probably had more knowledge of babies than the doctor delivering me. She didn't give up on me.

Dr. Parks, on the other hand, told my folks I would not live out the week. I was placed in an incubator. My first home had metal bars on the windows. I looked like a very small prisoner in the pictures from the hospital.

My paternal grandparents had been out of town the night I was born and rushed back on the news that their first grandchild may not make it. Upon seeing me in my incubator, turning my head, pressing up and looking around to see who had come to meet me, my grandmother told my father, "There's nothing wrong with that boy," she said. "That boy will live. He's strong." She was right of course. She was usually right about things like this.

It would be a month before I left the incubator, and my mother could hold me for the first time. I was a tiny little thing weighing a little over five pounds when I left the hospital, but I was alive! No longer dead or dying. I was the size of a doll, and just as breakable it would seem. But I would have to face much bigger dragons.

I would not be the first child my parents would have to bear the pangs of death, but I would certainly cause them to fear my death for many years to come. It would not be the last time death tried to steal my life. On more than one occasion I should have been dead by now, but for whatever reason, God has allowed me to continue living because he is not yet finished with my story.

One such occasion happened when I was in the fifth grade, I believe. We had been down at my grandparent's farm in Crews, Texas, which is the name of a small community that no longer exists. When I was a child, there was an old community schoolhouse building that was still standing. My grandmother told me that she graduated high school at that school. To look at it, you would have thought it was a dilapidated building, but for that small farming community, it was still the place people gathered for reunions. My grandmother attended her fiftieth school reunion there in 1988.

Back to my story, it was early fall. My grandfather had just finished cutting his alfalfa crop, and he was baling the hay. I loved to tag along with both him and my father, helping them grab the bales of hay and stack them on the trailer. By the end of the weekend, I was getting sick.

My parents loaded up the station wagon with me in the back on a pallet of blankets. I was coughing and running a fever. We headed back to Midland, and once we were home my folks put me to bed.

Sometime in the night my mom got up to check on me. I was having a difficult time breathing. I was wheezing terribly, and my mom was very worried. My parents had prayed over me. My folks wanted to have faith that I would overcome this and be fine without a doctor's help.

My father has never liked doctors. I think it stems from the fact that he was a very sick child, near death for many years, and he never has gotten over his dislike of doctors. Not because he does not like them, but because he would rather pray and seek a spiritual solution than to give up and seek medical help. This, however, was not something that seemed like it was going away easily.

Late that night, my folks packed me up, and we headed to the hospital. The doctors told my folks it was a good thing they came in when they did. I was thirty-minutes away from dying from the fluid that had built up in my lungs. I remember the doctor gave me a shot, and I threw up this nasty green bile. If you have ever seen a commercial for Mucinex with the green mucus monster that is what this looked like.

I was one very sick child, but God gave my mother the nudge she needed to insist my father take me to the hospital. That decision most likely saved my life for the second time, and again it involved my ability to breath. It took a medical professional to step in and perform the life-saving act. I am quite grateful for the doctors.

Another time I was gravely ill was in college. I was so very sick that my throat had swollen shut from inflammation. I had gone to the campus clinic for several weeks trying to get well. They issued me amoxicillin for the infection, but it never got better. Of course, I was continuing to party nearly every night so my body did not have time to heal, and the meds could not do the job intended with so much booze and so little sleep.

After a month of this, I wound up in the clinic running a fever, and I was delirious. My roommate, Rusty, took me because I could not walk or drive the three blocks to the clinic. The old doctor that was there decided that I was stable enough to stay at the clinic instead of a hospital. Even though he proved himself right, I was always upset with him for not sending me to the emergency room. Instead, he gave me a cup of boiling hot Mountain Dew to hold in my throat until the swelling subsided enough to swallow. He then made me take those amoxicillin pills again down my very raw throat.

I don't recall too much more from that stay in the infirmary other than going in and out of consciousness for several days. I remember passing out on the doctor's office table and becoming conscious again shortly afterward. Rusty would bring friends over to see me so that they could laugh at me for the way I would pass out, wake back up, and keep talking with me never knowing I had passed out. I was a mess.

I recall the doctor calling my mother and telling her that I was going to be just fine, and not to worry about me. Two days later, my grandparents came to town and checked on their boy. They tracked me down through Rusty to find me in a state of semi-consciousness. I know I worried them, but they were assured I would be okay.

For years, looking back on this experience, I was angry with my mother for not coming to rescue me. I was disappointed that I did not get the attention that I wanted. That disappointment would feed my insecurities. Because I was not living in alignment with the Heavenly Father and was living my life in a carnal way, I was simply reaping what I had sown in my life.

The doctor who treated me knew what I needed was to get some antibiotics and fluids in me and to rest. His insistence that I was going to be okay was based on years and years of experience dealing with drunk teenagers that did not have good life skills. He simply put me in my place, which was in a small room. No fancy medical equipment, no round the clock monitors beeping; just some basic medicine and some rest.

In essence, it was a medical spanking instead of the spa treatment. That was God showing me He loved me, but I was being rebellious and did not learn my lesson. My mother was doing all she could. She called and checked on me. I was nineteen years old, and I was an adult in the eyes of the law. She had a husband, a job, my sister and a five-year old son at home to care for. I was "adulting", and I was not very good at it.

Jesus' love for me is the only thing I can credit for the many, many times my life has been spared. In 1985, I left a gay bar in Odessa and drove back to Midland, which was about a thirty-minute drive. I had been drinking all night and was driving back when I blacked out.

I woke up with the car spinning. As I was entering the Midland city limits, I had gone off the road into soft sand from a new construction site off the loop access for Midland. I awoke to a nightmare before my very eyes. I could not control anything. The car was spinning at thirty or forty miles per hour when I went off the road. I watched as the car spun into a chain link fence surrounding a self-storage facility. I came to rest about ten feet from a huge commercial dumpster.

The car hit the fence and I survived. The vehicle looked like it had been in a demolition derby. The trunk was smashed so compactly that you could not open it, and the rear bumper was clear up to the gas cap. It's a complete miracle that the car did not explode, that I was not thrown out of the car, that I did not kill someone else, and most importantly that I did not hit the dumpster.

Remarkably, I drove the wrecked heap back to my apartment and escaped being picked up and arrested for drunk driving. God was watching out for me. I did not deserve the protection, but the army of God was on my side that night. The following day I had friends drive me by the scene of the wreck to survey the damage. Things didn't look too bad for the fence, but I had left behind a breadcrumb trail of evidence of broken glass, hubcaps, and parts of fenders. All of this was being collected by the police as we drove by to see how bad it was.

I remember thinking that I had gotten away with this and how lucky

I was. Luck had nothing to do with it. God spared me.

The following week I got a call from the local police department. They had issued me a ticket for failing to report a crime, for leaving the scene of a crime, and not reporting hitting a fixed object. I got a fine and went on down the road. My life did not change. I was still arrogant, and I would nearly repeat this same event nine years later.

I had been at my friend Tom's house, drinking champagne all afternoon. I had volunteered to pick up my friends, Lance and T.J., from the airport. I decided that I would bring a bottle of champagne with me so that we could all have a roadie on the way back to town.

Along the way, I ran off the road and side swiped the guard rail. The side of my car was all scraped up, but I was too drunk to tell how much damage I had done. I arrived at the airport, and my friends saw the car. They looked at me, and T.J. said to Lance, "What's wrong with Steve"? Lance said, "He's drunk. Can't you tell?"

That escapade garnered me a nickname that took years to lose, but even that did not change my way of living. I continued to drink and do drugs when driving for decades. My serial abuse of my life and taking other peoples' lives for granted blows me away when I look back on it now. I would have said I was not that bad of a drinker, but my record speaks for itself. It tells a much different story. One of bad decisions, bad choices, and Amazing Grace!

During my descent into drugs, I came close to overdosing many times. I recall one time in particular, I shot up so much crystal meth that I felt like my head was going to come off my body. This experience scared me, sending me into a spiral of guilt, shame, and regret; however, it would not last. I kept going back to drugs for many more years.

Each time, I would get my act together, and I thought I was getting better. I was able to stop, so therefore, I had no problem. This could not have been farther from the truth. I was a broken person that was trying to slap a band-aid on each time that I failed so I could just keep going down the road. I didn't realize it at the time, but I was just traveling further down the road to destruction.

It seemed like it was a nice road at times. I made new friends and I made good money. I bought expensive cars, jewelry, and artwork. I lived like a prince. The truth is, I was living like a prince, alright - a prince of darkness. It's odd saying that out loud, but that is exactly what my life had become. I was living a lie. I looked successful to the world, but I was just a fraud. The person people met was living like a dead man.

The life I was living at that time had all the trappings of a good life, but there was very little good in my life. I had the ability to attract people just like myself: broken souls that needed healing. That is not a bad thing as far as Christians go. Our duty to love one another is paramount.

However, being in gay relationships meant disobedience to God. For that reason alone, any love I gave or received from another man in a romantic or sexual way was counter to God's plan for my life. Therefore, that love relationship was invalid, and in effect, the love voided upon delivery.

While living as a gay man, I was giving love to other men that was not holy. Only within the bounds of a heterosexual relationship can that love become holy because God established that relationship from the beginning. That does not mean that gay people cannot express love, and it does not mean that within the gay community that love for God and love expressed from one individual to another in brotherly love is invalid.

What it means is that the romantic emotional bond that is eternal does not exist in a gay relationship. It cannot. God does not recognize that as his purpose for your life; therefore, any relationship - straight or gay - that is purely based upon sexual gratification will always fail.

Most gay romantic relationships, at some point, are based solely on the sexual attraction to another person. That false sexual attraction is what invalidates God's holiness in the relationship. It does not make God unholy because he cannot become unholy. He already died for the sins of man. He is righteous, and for us to be righteous, we must live as he instructed us to live. Any life outside those bounds will be a life lost unless it changes its course.

I believe that one of the root causes of the sin of homosexuality in my life was self-centeredness. I wanted what I wanted at any cost. I hurt many people along the way and destroyed people's lives. I did not care about others if I could get my way. The funny thing is people will tell you what a kind person I was, and how thoughtful and generous I was. Those things are true, but I also was thoughtless and selfish.

When it came down to it, I had always put myself first. I didn't see it. I couldn't see it. I was a victim of myself, living proof of my fallen sinful man, man-made destruction, a walking talking disaster about to explode at any moment. When I finally did explode, I hurt people badly, and then wondered why they didn't love me.

I am sometimes surprised that anyone ever loved me, as I was not very lovable. I did not see how destructive I was. The narcissistic side of me, the side that wanted and desired every pleasure I could get my hands on, clouded my vision. I saw the good in me but not the bad. That lack of perspective allowed me to continue in my sin, even when I would acknowledge in my inner being that homosexuality was wrong.

Yet, I still fought this and found ways to support my position. I found literature that backed up my argument and surrounded myself with like-minded people that believed what I tried to convince myself I believed.

The truth was that I never fully believed it. I knew the Truth. I was living contrary to my Creator's plans for my life, and each road I would travel down would require more of myself to keep going. When I first started down the road of homosexuality, I needed booze and cigarettes to help me navigate my uneasiness. Getting past my conviction and shame required a numbing agent.

The longer I traveled down the road, the stronger the numbing agent became. I needed to be heavily medicated to deal with the lie I was living. The guilt, shame, and pain I felt was a heavy burden to carry. I was trying to carry it all alone.

This weight was like a millstone around my neck. It weighed me down and caused me real, physical pain. By 2005, I suffered from constant low back pain from a herniated disc. I had arthritis and bone spurs in my back from the brittle bones in my back. By 2013 I was in pain twenty-four hours a day, seven days a week unless I was on Hydrocodone. I was completely hooked on them.

It would not be long before they were not enough. I would need alcohol mixed with the pills to numb the pain, and when that did not work, I used cocaine and crystal meth. Both would lead me into more and more risky sex and putting my life in danger with the individuals I was associating with.

I was ashamed of myself, but I was not willing to give anything up. I would push the pause button for a while on the street drugs. That would keep the risky sex at bay, but I knew the rush of the poison and the thrill of being out of control. This is something that I had become addicted to, the momentary escape from reality. It never lasted. I would quickly become paranoid, my actions would be erratic, and I would need more drugs to compensate for that feeling, too.

My life was unraveling, and so, I decided I needed to do something to cement it. In 2016, gay marriage became legal in the United States. I was in a relationship with a man, and although we had never really expressed any desire to marry, the financial benefits of marriage were an issue that we discussed often. Marriage would afford us a more comfortable lifestyle with less cash going out the door each month.

Now, I really didn't like the idea of gay marriage, but as they say, when in Rome... I realized I didn't know if I could even go through with marrying someone again. My first marriage had been so disastrous in my mind, that I had no good feelings about marriage. In addition, I had been in so many failed relationships that I didn't know what to expect of marriage at this stage of life.

My relationship with Jon was one that looked good from the outside by the world's standards and at this point I had decided that this relationship was to be my final one. I had settled on Jon. We had a lovely home and nice cars, we had lots of friends, and we liked to travel. Our life had the appearance of being a very happy relationship, but the truth was much darker.

Early on in our relationship, drugs came into the picture, and it would soon require drugs to have sex. Everything about the relationship that was personal, and intimate was dependent on drugs, fantasy with porn, S&M, and bondage. This was a very different relationship than that of my parents or grandparents. This was drunk and disorderly, full of fights and disloyalty.

I was the one that demanded my way in everything. I was the most self-centered, narcissistic person I knew how to be. Yet, in the fall of 2016, when Jon proposed the idea that we were going to get married I did not object. Now the odd thing is Jon never asked me to marry him. He just announced to our friends that we were getting married, and I ran with it and planned a wedding in four months. This was the basis for our marriage - everything was hurried.

I was a mess. My serial abuse of sex and drugs was becoming a topic among our friends. Our life, mine especially, was nothing short of a hurricane heading to town, and we were getting married. This was not a wise decision, and it was one that I had to convince myself to go through with.

Jon had family that would object, but we convinced them to participate. I was certain my family would not show up, but to my surprise they all did. I managed to pull off a big wedding with a nice reception. Everything was done in style, everything looked good from the outside, but problems had begun to surface again just before the wedding.

A few weeks before the wedding, I went off on a bender, and my problem was bad enough to cause my dad to come check on me. He tried to convince me that I might want to cancel the wedding, but I was not about to listen to him. I was going to pick myself back up and do it. I was going through with it, full steam ahead. It would not take long for the train to go off the tracks for good. This time I would leave a wave of destruction in my wake.

After a year, our relationship had gone downhill so badly. Even so, on our first anniversary we went to New York City to celebrate. It was not a happy trip. We fought most of the time. It was the most miserable vacation I've ever been on.

New York City at Christmas time is a fascinating place, full of wonderful sights and sounds, but we spent little time enjoying the good things and most of the time searching for things of no real value. I came back ready for a divorce, but I didn't know how I would be able to afford one. Things had gotten so messed up, so much was invested in this relationship, and the health insurance benefit was something I desperately needed.

I was stuck it seemed, in a very unhappy relationship, but fortunately, there were drugs to numb me. I would go deeper and deeper into them, until I had caused a fracture in my relationship with Jon, and he wanted out. That was what I wanted all along, I suppose. I wanted to be discarded, so I could blame someone else for my problems.

The truth is that upon reflection, I have discovered that the one common denominator in all my failed relationships is me. I am the one that entered into each one of them, and I was a party to each and every failed relationship.

The one relationship that had never been fully severed was my relationship with the Lord. I had placed Him in last place, far behind everything else. I would dust Him off in my hour of need or my desire to get better, but I was only going through the motions of being a believer. I was not willing to completely give myself over to Christ and allow him to work in me until I had hit rock bottom.

My rock bottom occurred in the fall of 2018. I had moved out of the house I shared with Jon and was living in a small one-bedroom apartment. My apartment was everything I needed in more ways than I would know at the time. Because of my finances, I was forced to find an apartment I could afford with a property that would take me with my bad credit. The nicest one was in Odessa, and for a Midland boy, it was sacrilege to move to Odessa. However, I made the move, and I loved my little 700 square foot apartment.

I was getting back on my feet from the breakup with Jon. At least, it looked like I was, but the truth was that I had landed in the lions' den…and it was just where I wanted to be.

Odessa was full of drugs and druggies. Sex was easy to come by when you had drugs, and it wasn't long before I was at the end of my rope. I know there had to be many people praying for me. If there had not been people praying, I would probably not still be here.

God sent me two angels to steer me towards Him. One was named Barbara, and the other was named Michael. Barbara was the parish priest at our local Episcopal Church in Midland, and Michael was a former drug dealer that had gotten sober and was running a sober house in a Drug Treatment facility.

Barbara came to see me and took me to lunch. All the while, I was freaking out thinking that there was about to be an intervention. There was, I just didn't know it was spiritual. Michael reached out to me and asked if I was ok. I told him what was going on, and he told me to pray. I said that I don't even know how to pray anymore, and he told me that if I could not pray that he would pray for me.

That kindness from these two people put me on course for a spiritual renewal that would forever change my life. They didn't know each other. They did not coordinate their plans. It was all God working His plan out for my life and my way back to him.

STEVEN STEHLE

CHAPTER XVIII

THE ROAD BACK HOME

In the fall of 2018, I had finally hit my rock bottom. I wanted off the road that I had been heading down. The end of the road was coming. I could see how it would all end if I continued down the road with drugs, and finally I wanted help. I wanted it badly. After Barbara had come to see me and showed me the love of God, I began to have enough courage and strength to admit my problem to myself and to my family.

It was not a surprise to anyone that I was an addict, but I was now willing to try and break free of the addiction. I knew that La Hacienda in Hunt, Texas was the best rehab facility in the country, and I knew that if I could get back there, I could finally find a way to break free of the drugs. I had been down this road before, and I knew it led to life. Though I had never completed the journey, I knew what lay ahead.

"Therefore, since Christ suffered in his body, arm yourselves also with the same attitude, because he who has suffered in his body is done with sin. As a result, he does not live the rest of his earthly life for evil human desires, but rather for the will of God. For you have spent enough time in the past doing what pagans choose to do—living in debauchery, lust, drunkenness, orgies, carousing and detestable idolatry."
1 Peter 4: 1-3 (NIV).

Getting into La Hacienda was not easy. They had a spot for me, but my insurance did not want to pay. The fight to get into rehab was a battle that my life depended on, and I was not willing to give up. I spent two weeks fighting with insurance, hoping, and waiting for an answer that I would finally be approved. That answer came the week before Thanksgiving of 2018.

At this time, I had been drug-free for two weeks, but I knew I needed more than to just dry out. I needed help in rebuilding my life. When I got the approval to go, I was very excited and nervous at the same time. This meant change. I am usually pretty good with change, but I like to know what kind of change I am walking into. This is not one of those situations. When you make a commitment to really change your life you have to actually deal with yourself and what has brought you down your road of destruction.

I had been staying with my folks in Brady while I waited for the okay to come to La Ha. When it came, I drove myself to rehab. That is not the normal course of events for addicts. Most addicts are forced into rehab by family, friends, work, or the threat of jail time. For me, it was a choice.

As I drove down to Hunt, Texas, I was listening to worship music on my satellite radio station. As I drove, I began to pray and beg God to restore me. My words were pleading with Him to restore me. I was in tears, like a flood. I was completely overwhelmed by the love of God in that moment. For me personally, my road to Damascus was a state highway from Brady, Texas to Hunt, Texas. I met the Lord on that road while driving and praying and asking for His help. I asked Him to completely restore me.

Now, that is a bold request. In that moment, I knew it might mean that I would no longer be gay, but I did not care. I just wanted to be healed. That road trip is one of my most treasured memories. I was alone except for the Holy Spirit. The two of us re-established our relationship one with another. I acknowledged His presence and began to receive the love that was a gift from God and was able to feel the real tangible presence of His spirit.

When the Spirit moved and touched me it was very real. My body was able to sense His presence, and that intimate personal interaction is almost indescribable. The sensation of tingling life flowing inside your body is like being struck by lightning. You would expect the hair on your arms to stand up! That is how very real and personal His presence is. His spirit made me weep with joy.

A joy that is completely overwhelming and to anyone who has never experienced it difficult to explain. The joy of the Lord is peace, love, and strength, but it is so much more.

Upon arriving at La Ha, I checked myself in and went through the process of signing my life away to my new captors. It's funny to say it that way, but in a real sense that is what admitting yourself to rehab is like. You admit your need for correction, your need to be redeemed and reformed. This is the time that you show up and turn yourself over to the sheriff, admitting you're a wanted man, and asking that the judge be lenient towards you since you did the honorable thing and gave yourself up.

That is the very best way I can describe the decision to choose to go to rehab. It's saying I'm a wanted man, that God has a price on my head, and I don't want to end up in a pine box because there is a bounty out for me dead or alive. But I was full of pride for my decision to do this on my own. I didn't realize it at the time, but on reflection, I can see how proud I was of myself. I was fourteen days sober. I was choosing to make a change in my life, but I had no idea what was about to happen to me in making that choice.

The first thing I had to do was pay up. I had to part with money and pay the down payment on my future. It was $2,700.00, and I was fortunate enough to have that kind of money in the bank. Not many druggies have that kind of money lying around. The next thing I had to do was be evaluated. Someone had to examine me and determine what my addictions were. In essence, I had to be strip searched and give blood and urine to establish a baseline on my life. This is somewhat shameful. It strips you down and exposes you for who you are, to the point of being a medical problem that needs help. I saw this as just a means to an end until I had my first unpleasantness.

Upon taking the urine test, the nurse came back and said the test shows your high on amphetamines. I was outraged! I had not taken any methamphetamines. I was fourteen days sober, and there was no way any drugs were in my system. I was incensed that she would accuse me of still using.

The funny thing is that I was still using legal drugs to address problems in my life. Drugs that would show up as a false positive. In no way was I abusing, but it still made me feel shame and it caused me to get angry. This anger was not the right response as it just kept me open to other things. If I had been more contrite and less full of self-pride, I might have just said I guess the drugs are taking a long time to flush out of my body. The reaction of anger was all out of pride, and that pride would be an issue that would have to be dealt with over and over again.

Once I had been medically approved to enter rehab, I was placed in a waiting room until my luggage and personal items could be searched, inventoried, and prohibited items seized. This is humiliating, but I understand how necessary it is. This process is for your safety and the safety of others, but it is also a part of the breaking down of personal space. The process of establishing who is in control, and it isn't you. During the wait, I sat in the small kitchen in the hospital area of the facility where they hold you until they figure out where to place you.

While I was there, a couple of other people were admitted as well. One of these people was a young lady named Jill. We barely met and hardly said a word to each other because it's not a happy place as you would imagine. During that time, a young man came to join us. He was full of arrogance, reeked of booze, and was obviously still drunk. He tried to hit on every woman he saw. It was like watching a movie and knowing the outcome. I knew he was going to be trouble.

Jill and I just looked at each other, shook our heads, and said he's still drunk. He even admitted that he had the taxi driver stop at the liquor store along the way to be sure and get one last party on the way to rehab. Does that sound familiar? I did the same thing when I tried to get clean in 2004. Party it up like the world is about to end.

I didn't know it at the time, but this time things would really be different for me, and it would involve Jill. God had planned it out to the very day and moment that I arrived that she and I would meet. God had something planned for me that would require a Jill to show me how much He loved me. His plans for me had already been made. I was just following through with what He ordained, and it all began with my decision to give Him back the power in my life.

During my stay at La Ha in 2018, God provided me with so many blessings, almost on a daily basis. This time around the atmosphere seemed different, but the surroundings were the same. The beauty of the Texas Hill Country with a fall morning sunrise is a magical moment. The people I met were from all different walks of life, and each person added something to the experience. Some were good, some not so good; however, the perspective that I had gained coming back this time changed how I viewed others and myself and my ability to finally get the help I needed to get clean and change my life.

Group counseling is one of the best tools I can recommend for someone struggling with addiction. If you can find a safe place to express yourself and listen to what other people have to say about how they view your actions, it's a life changing experience. Unfortunately, many people in rehab only go through the motions to please someone else.

In my experience, taking Jesus Christ out of the picture and substituting a vague idea of a higher power is a recipe for failure. Being at a place like La Ha that provides some spiritual tools really does help. I'm thankful that many of the counselors I met were Christians. They helped me find the right spiritual tools. As I said earlier in this book, I take issue with twelve-step programs that take God out and replace Him with a higher power. I have seen first-hand how badly this can go.

Once I heard someone describe their higher power as a pink unicorn riding a bicycle. I've heard teachers say you can choose anything to be your higher power: the earth, trees, the moon, the stars or a little dog named Toto. It's all too convenient for someone who is struggling with addiction to make a lousy choice and be stuck in a rut of going in and out of treatment and in and out of sobriety. Thankfully for me LaHa was a very nurturing place that helped build up my spiritual connections.

One of the many wonderful experiences I had at rehab in 2018 is the blessing that God provided on Thanksgiving Day. This time at rehab my folks did not visit every week. The rules had changed. I had not planned on arriving during Thanksgiving, and no plans for family to come and spend the day with me had been made; however, there were plenty of other people in the same boat as me. Being without family on a holiday is rather difficult for anyone dealing with addiction.

Fortunately for me, God had big plans for me that day. Remember the woman named Jill? Well, her family came to visit her for Thanksgiving, and when anyone has a holiday in rehab it can be stressful for the family. They are forced to try and act like nothing is wrong. All the while the lives of everyone around them is falling apart.

Jill's life was no different. Her home life was going through some real struggles, and her children and husband looked to be doing their best to just hold it together. As I sat in the art room working on rope bracelets, Jill brought her children in to see what we were doing and to see if they wanted to paint a rock or make a bracelet…anything to pass the uncomfortable time of being in an uncomfortable place.

Now it just so happened that Jill also had three children. She had two boys and a girl, and they were about the same ages my children had been when I got my divorce. The most amazing thing is that each of her children had first names that started with a "J", just like mine.

The middle child, a boy named Jager, came and sat in my lap and asked me to show him how to make rope bracelets. I got to play daddy for an hour on Thanksgiving Day, 2018. As I looked across the table at Jill, we both started to cry. She knew my story and knew how special this was to me. She knew of my son Jaret, and that I had lost him. She knew that Jager was about the same age my son was when I divorced, and that in that moment it was as if God had dropped down from Heaven and gave me an hour of time with Jaret again.

God blessed me in a way in which I could not have asked for. The only opportunity I would have to experience this gift was to be submissive to His will, to seek Him and to fight for my restoration. My decision to ask God to restore me opened a door to all kinds of blessings I was soon to experience. It all started with my decision to bend my will to His, to ask for him to change me and for me to be willing to change…not with words but actions.

Another gift God gave me while at rehab was the gift of faith. He restored faith that I had lost. One of the examples of that is His spirit encouraging me to pray for strangers and friends alike. On one occasion in a group meeting, a young lady that was sitting next to me, Nancy, leaned over and told me she was having really bad cravings to use drugs at that moment.

I knew her story about her drug use, her desire to get clean, and start her life over. I knew that she was a believer but was struggling with her faith through all that she had gone through. She asked me to pray for her. I laid hands on her and said a little prayer out loud asking God to calm the cravings she was having and to give her peace.

Afterwards while we sat next to each other, I said a silent prayer and asked God to allow the Holy Spirit to show her how much she is loved. Later in the meeting, she had a noticeable change in her attitude. She was suddenly very involved in the meeting.

After the meeting broke up, I asked her how she was feeling. She told me that after I prayed for her, while she was sitting there next to me, she felt a bolt of lightning shoot through her body. She knew it was the Holy Spirit, and all her cravings went away.

For the remainder of time I was there, I saw a new creature in her. She had begun to change before my eyes. She was at peace for the first time since she had arrived. All of this happened while I was still a self-professing gay man. You see, the label I had placed on myself was not the label that God saw. He did not see a gay man. He saw a son He loved. He saw Jesus reflected in me. I was a new creation in Christ, and that is the only label He saw.

From that moment on, I began to choose that label of forgiveness. That was who I was - my new name was *Forgiven*. I am a new creature in Christ Jesus. I am one with Him.

After I left rehab, I went back to my parents to help with an estate sale we were conducting for a family. That opportunity gave me the chance to meet many people in my parents' hometown of Brady. These people welcomed me into their lives without judgment. Many knew of my struggles with addiction and most everyone knew that I was a gay man. That did not change how they treated me or viewed me. They showed me love.

For the first time in decades, I saw the church of God that was reaching beyond its self-imposed boundaries of acceptance. One of the biggest flaws I have seen in the church is the idea that sinners should somehow not be allowed into fellowship with "believers". This is in direct opposition to the whole basis and design of the work of Christ in the life of man.

Christ never qualified who He ministered to or whom He allowed into His fellowship outside of the choice to follow Him. He knew that when he chose twelve disciples that He was choosing flawed men. These twelve came with all the selfish desires of man, all the fears of man, and all the failures of the carnal man. He did not ask for perfect men. He asked for believers.

The only way anyone becomes a believer is by being exposed to other believers unless God miraculously comes down and confronts him. The life of a Christian is one of service, not judgment and of faith, not a haughty attitude of superiority. We all are born with a sinful nature and have fallen short of the mark.

No one has ever been created without sin other than Christ Jesus. He is the example. He is what we strive to attain in our lives. Without the help of the Holy Spirit inside us, we are just blindly walking through life trying to do good or choosing to go our own way. Either way, we are not - and cannot - be made perfect without Him. To see ourselves as better than others is in itself blasphemous.

I believe that the addict has given in to all his passions. I believe that God has shown me that all addiction is rooted in sin, and that most sin is an addiction to self. We, by nature, are addicted to certain things in life. Our carnal man finds the things that please him, and in pleasure, there is opportunity to sin.

That choice to sin is free will, and all addiction is through free will. People will say that certain addictions are caused by a medical problem, and to a certain extent they are, but they have a basis in something. Even if you are born with that inclination to alcohol or drugs or sexual immorality or homosexuality, it is not something that you do without a choice.

Every person that has dealt with these issues has been at a crossroad at some point in his life, and yet chooses to keep going down that path, else he chooses to walk away. That choice is the empirical evidence of the fact that an addiction to self has given way to a lifestyle or drug or alcohol problem that did not exist until that choice was made.

Some choices are made in subtle ways that don't even seem like choices to us when we are young, but they open us up to powers greater than ourselves: spirits that will influence us. Once we start down that slippery slope it takes more than just will power to overcome those evil spirits. It takes the power and authority of Jesus Christ in us, which is over all unclean spirits.

When we are baptized into the life of Christ, we automatically acquire all the authority that was given Him over this world. Ephesians 4:22-24 (NAS) says,

> *"That in reference to your former manner of life, you lay aside the old self, which is being corrupted in accordance with the lust of deceit, and that you be renewed in the spirit of your mind, and put on the new self which in the likeness of God has been created in righteousness and holiness of the truth."*

Ephesians 6:12 (KJV) says,

> *"For we wrestle not with flesh and blood, but against*

principalities, against powers, against the rulers of the darkness of this world, against spiritual wickedness in high places."

This means that when we are wrestling with our addictions, even though they are manifested in the physical, they are based in the spiritual. Our spiritual weakness has given rise to a physical manifestation in our lives. We become weak and dependent on the things that please our flesh.

I want to be clear and say I am not saying that everything that pleases us is bad or is somehow sinful. What I am saying is that we know in our spirit when we have crossed that line into the ungodly. We have a switch inside us that gets flipped on, and when it does, we become aware of our sin. That is the nature of sin. It bares itself in us. We are aware we have sinned, and then we choose to either fight it or give in to sin. Once we have chosen to give into a specific sin, then we become partakers in the army of Satan without our knowledge.

One way I became aware of this in my life is when I was walking in homosexuality. I spent much of my time in gay bars and went to gay events that championed gay causes. I rode on the Imperial Float of the Gay Pride Parade in New York City in the year 2001. That, in itself, should have said it all to me. I had crowned myself as a gay man, and I was promoting it on the world stage, saying, "Look at me!"

The gay flag, or the rainbow flag, is intended to be a symbol of pride...pride that is not justified in the eyes of God. There is pride that is justified like pride of country or pride of parents. Pride of homosexuality is not legitimate pride and therefore is bound to cause destruction. The old saying pride goes before the fall is quite true.

In Ezekiel Chapter 1, the prophet Ezekiel is describing the image of God that he saw when Heaven opened up before him. In Ezekiel 1:28 (NLT) he states,

> *"All around him was a glowing halo, like a rainbow shining in the clouds on a rainy day. This is what the glory of the Lord looked like to me."*

The rainbow, which is the image of the glory of God, was given to humanity by God as a symbol of His love for us. It was done after the fall, in the great flood. God gave Noah a promise that He would never destroy the earth with water again. To prove his covenant with man, He gave us the rainbow as an enduring emblem of this promise.

The rainbow is not a symbol of pride to be used to wave in God's face and say, "Look at me! Here I am!" It is a covenant with man showing that God's love and His promises are everlasting. Man has taken a sacred covenant and turned it into a false flag, celebrating gay pride. This is perhaps one of the most disrespectful things I can imagine outside of disrespecting the cross.

When God gives His word, He keeps it. When we choose to make fun of it or appropriate the imagery of His promise for things that go in direct conflict with His will, we are saying to Him that we choose ourselves over God, and in this case the objective of L.G.B.T.Q. is to glorify themselves with the image of the glory of God. This is an affront to God and His promises.

The world we live in is broken, and most people are living in some form of sin. To identify someone else's sin as sinful, just because it is not the same as your sin, means that you have set yourself above others. That is not your job to do.

We become one with Christ, and we are seated with Him, but He first had to come down and join Himself with us. So, we are all made one with Him. For us all to be one, that means that we need to see sinners as parts of the body that need redemption. Otherwise, we are choosing to eliminate part of the body that God intends to use.

We must strive to be actively engaged in caring for all the body of Christ which is all of humanity. One day we will have to give an account of how we cared for and loved our fellow man. That is the greatest commandment, that you love one another as yourself. If we do not love our fellow man, but reject him, we are rejecting parts of ourselves. Our mission is one of love!

Once I was back home in Odessa I started to try and put my old world back together in some format that allowed me to make changes and to continue down the road to restoration. I did not know for certain what that would look like. In the back of my mind, I had been struggling with the identity of being gay. I tried to walk back into the same groups of friends that I still had when I went to rehab. Some of these people would continue to be friends and others would not.

The biggest change started when I decided to stop smoking cigarettes. Somewhere in the back of my mind some twenty or thirty years ago, I had the thought that if I ever quit smoking, I would not be gay anymore. Somehow my ability to live as a gay man was challenged by stopping smoking.

That may sound like a funny thing, but that was the Holy Spirit that was inside me telling me that I was addicted to cigarettes and that the addiction to cigarettes was connected to all the other issues in my life. I had been living a life that I chose to smoke, and in that choice, I gave permission for other forces to work in my life. I had opened a door to homosexuality in my youth and with cigarettes I had left that door opened. If I chose to stop smoking, I could shut a door to that influence in my life.

In doing so, I soon found gay relationships to be a struggle. After giving up cigarettes, I found that when I drank alcohol I could lose my judgement, and I could make bad decisions that would lead me to choices that I would regret with men. All of this was the Holy Spirit working for me. I had given the Holy Spirit permission to restore me, and by doing that, He started pointing out the things in my life that I should change in order to have a full, open relationship with the Father.

The Father desired me to be in fellowship with Him. That is what he created me for, but as long as I was living a certain way, I was impeding my access to the Father. My access had not been denied, but the power that He wished to impart to my life was diminished by my continued walk down the road that had doorways to homosexuality. The only way for me to finally walk in complete peace and allow Him to work His plan for me in my life was for me to bend my will further to His will.

I had to make a full one hundred eighty degree change in my life. I had to start making choices based on how things impacted my relationship with the Father. Once I started making those choices, I felt freedom I had never experienced before. Joy that is beyond words filled my soul. I was now overflowing with joy, hope, and love; that joy, that hope, and love gave me the power to continue to change.

In miraculous timing, God restored things in my life that I had tried desperately on my own to change. I suddenly had a job with benefits. I began to have financial means and opportunities that had not been there before. God was blessing me in things I didn't even know how to ask for. He was piece by piece restoring order to my life and blessing me because He loves me.

The Father loves me. Jesus loves me. I know it's true because He gave me His Holy Spirit living within me that testifies to me of His undying love.

Looking back over my life, I can see so many times God showed up and rescued me. That is a testament to his love, grace, and mercy. The times He showed His love for me in subtle ways are now precious memories. God's grace has been extended many more times than I can count, and His mercy in my life is without question.

One of the more important things that God did for me in light of my son's death was the gift of peace that he provided to me before Jaret's death. In the weeks preceding our move from Abilene to Midland, the people that Zach worked for had a going away party for him. The two lesbians that owned the health food store where Zach worked had thrown a lovely party to say goodbye. Jaret went with us, and this was the first time any of these people had met him.

One of the ladies was a founding member of the M.C.C. churches and a leader in gay Christian circles. I had known of her from my days in Dallas and had just come to know her in Abilene through her purchase of the health food store.

At this party, she had invited a straight couple that had an evangelistic ministry in the Abilene area, and the man was speaking to my son at the party. I was busy going from room to room and saying hello to all the guests when I happened to walk past the room Jaret and the evangelist were in. I heard the man ask Jaret if he was saved. I had never thought to ask my son this question. I was too busy with my silly life to pay attention to this very important factor in my child's life, but this stranger took the time to ask.

I listened as Jaret told the account of how he was saved at a bible camp as a teenager, and how he had been baptized and saved. This small detail in the life of my son would be the most important gift that God gave me regarding the life of my son. Knowing that Jaret had made the choice to follow God, that he had answered the call, and had opened the door to Christ was the one thing that I would need in order to have peace in Jaret's death. I didn't know that Jaret would be dead in less than three months.

I did not know much about my son, but God knew. He also knew that this small detail was something that would give me much comfort. This was a gift He could offer me in opening a window into my son's life that was to be cut short. You see God already knew the outcome of Jaret's life. He had paved the way for me to have a relationship with him in the last days of his life. He had shown me that my son, though struggling with sin as all of us do, was chosen, loved, and embraced by the Father, and that no matter what, nothing could separate him from the love of God.

In this instance, it would take people that many other Christians would disapprove of to be the agents of God's hand in showing me His grace and mercy. I have seen time and time again how God has used everyone in my life, no matter who they were, to accomplish His purpose in my life and to show his love for me.

When I was a kid there was a slogan in commercials on TV and in magazines that said, "If it feels good do it." It was an attitude towards life that you should be free to do anything you like. That attitude is basically called rebellion. It is one that would cause me to stumble most of my life.

Even while writing this, I can feel the hand of Satan trying to tempt me with carnal pleasures that I spent years giving myself over too. You see, sin is not always something that you do against another person but what you do that affects your personal relationship with God the Father.

For me, I have struggled with masturbation my entire life. The desire can be so overwhelming that I don't think I will be able to overcome it some days, but the reality is that I can do all things through Christ who strengthens me! Masturbation is just a symptom of being out of perfect alignment with God. If I choose to do whatever pleases me at any moment, there is no telling what that inclination might develop into.

All sin is wrapped up in self. If I give into self, I am giving into sin and choosing myself and my will over God's will for my life. The act of masturbation may not seem like a big deal to some people. I am not killing anyone or stealing from anyone. I am not hurting anyone other than myself, but that is the point. I am hurting myself.

When I choose my will over God's will, I hurt myself by breaking the bond between us. Then, I am forced to repair that bond in order to maintain that bond of fellowship. It is not God the Father that walks away when I commit a sin, it is me that turns and walks away.

That selfish desire, whatever it is, puts distance between God and me. No matter how small the distance, it is one my soul is aware of.

Being out of fellowship, even for a few minutes or hours, is something that grieves my spirit and causes me to feel guilt and shame, guilt and shame that the Father never wants me to feel about myself. Therefore, if I confess my sins and tell the father what my struggles are, He is able to give me the strength to sustain me in the battle over my flesh. My flesh is weak for certain, and that is because it is flesh, not spirit. I am trying to keep my flesh in line with my spirit, and that battle is one that I cannot win on my own.

I want peace in my life, and that peace is found in a relationship with God the Father. That relationship requires that I have communication with Him on a regular basis. I must be able to say these are my struggles and these are my fears. Being able to have that open, honest dialog with the Father is what brings peace.

God is not a wishing well. If we only ever seek Him when we want something or are so desperate for something, we are not able to get His attention in the right way. It's like a child that never wants to mind. They keep saying, "Why, why, why," instead of, "Yes, sir!"

That rebellion causes the Father to discipline His children. One way He does this is by putting His kids in *time out*, spiritually speaking. He says, "Enough. Go to your room until you want to listen. I'm not going to listen to your childish temper tantrums."

When He does this, He often is trying to break your will and get you to realize that His yoke is much easier and that He has your best interest at heart, but that you must listen to Him and follow His commandments.

STEVEN STEHLE

CHAPTER XIV

AWAKENING

In the fall of 2019, I was at dinner with one of my nieces. In the little restaurant, the T.V. in the corner played a Disney series I had never seen before. As we were eating, I saw two teenage boys kissing on T.V. in a restaurant in my little west Texas town.

To say I was shocked is putting it mildly. I said with astonishment to my niece that the Disney show has two gay boys kissing. To which she said, "Oh, yeah." The next words out of her mouth made me even more uncomfortable. She said, "How does that make you feel?"

I couldn't answer her. She knew that it had taken me by surprise. How does that make me feel? Well, I'll tell you how it made me feel. It made me very uncomfortable. In that moment, I knew that I wasn't really comfortable with being gay. I had just been living a part in a very disturbing and complicated melodrama called my life.

Over the next few months, I slowly began to change. I knew for quite some time that I did not like the way gay people were being portrayed. The drag queen lifestyle, the leather lifestyle, and the party lifestyle were all things that I no longer felt comfortable allowing into my life. I knew not all gay people lived lives of depravity, but I began to see how each step down the path in my life had led to so much destruction.

It wasn't like I changed overnight from straight to gay. In the beginning, once the roots of homosexuality got planted, they spread like weeds in my life, and it would take lots of weeding the garden of my mind to remove them.

During the days to come, I would have worship music playing. I read my bible and prayed, and I began to pray for others' needs and not just my own. I thanked God for the many, many blessings He had bestowed upon me, the grace that He had shown me, and the unending, undeniable, everlasting love that had surrounded me and protected me from harm. I had come so close to death, so many times, but each time God allowed me to live. He wasn't finished with me yet, and my story was not yet written.

One day, after having seen a picture of my daughter Jade with her newborn child, and my son Jason with his new wife and children, my heart began to heal. I still don't have a relationship with them, but my spirit does. God has granted me the gift of sight, seeing their joy and happiness, knowing that God's plan for their lives is still to come.

I felt peace I had not experienced in decades. The last such time I had felt the peace of God come and envelope me was when my son Jaret died. In the midst of the storm that followed, upon discovering his lifeless body, and all the pain, turmoil, rejection, and anger that was aimed at me, I had been protected by the Holy Spirit. As I tell people, it was like walking on air. I was surrounded by the love of God, and all the arrows that were slung at me did not land on me. I was protected. It was such a supernatural experience of God's love, and I felt it so clearly.

May 12, 2020 marked ten years since Jaret died. The milestone was a big one. Like the stone that was rolled away when Christ was risen from the grave, I also had finally risen from my grave of pain, sorrow, addiction, jealousy, and deceit to finally be able to walk away from homosexuality.

Each time I tell a little story of my life, it takes the power away from it. I'm not rejoicing in my past. I'm grieving it and releasing the power of Christ that is within me to do battle for me and not against me.

The past few nights, after having spent the day writing this, I have been drained of energy and felt like I have been battling something. I realized it wasn't allergies, Covid-19, or any of the many other issues that try to steal my joy. No, this was something supernatural that was going on. I was in the midst of a great battle, and I hadn't realized it was still going on.

I was awakened from my sleep last night with a song in my head: "This is my story, this is my song, praising my savior all the day long. This is my story, this is my song, praising my savior all the day long."

As I began to sing along with this old Baptist hymn, I began to see in the darkness of my mind a multitude of people. I could not see faces, just shadows, and there was such peace. These people, the spirits that had been praying for my surrender and escape from homosexuality were there to rejoice. I was overcome by such love, grace, and acceptance at the thought that multitudes of angels were there to witness what was happening in my life and to stand beside me and battle with me to overcome my past and to march to victory.

One thing I want to stress is that life on the other side of the rainbow is beautiful. I have had to face many personal demons to find my peace, but the road was worth it. I know myself better than I ever have. I have "found myself", which is to say I found Jesus in me, and His spirit that lives inside me is the very breath I breathe.

The joy of being complete in Him is greater than any joy I ever found doing drugs or drinking. The confidence of having a friend that will never leave me, and a love that is pure that does not judge me for my weakness but uses it to write the story of His grace, love, and mercy is so profoundly mind blowing; so much so that I find it hard to express how deep and wide the breadth of His love is and how overwhelmed I am at the embrace of His love.

John 3:16 still applies to everyone. There is no one so lost or hurt or dirty that he cannot save him.

In John 4:10 (NLT), when Jesus spoke to the Samaritan woman who was under such a burden of sin, He said,

> *"If you only knew the gift God has for you and who you are speaking to you would ask me, and I would give you living water."*

The Living Water that wells up from within you is the Holy Spirit. You have the ability to draw from that well all the life-giving grace, mercy, peace and love that can heal any wound.

When I am in the presence of the Lord and His spirit falls on me, I know it. I can't help but weep for joy. That sense of peace and joy is my wish, hope, and prayer for each person that reads this book. If you do not know Christ as your Lord and Savior, if you have never experienced a personal relationship with Jesus, I am here to say:

"Come! The banquet has been set. The party is about to begin, and you are the guest of honor. Jesus is waiting!"

> *"And this is my prayer: that your love may abound more and more in knowledge and depth of insight. So that you may be able to discern what is best and may be pure and blameless*

until the day of Christ, filled with the fruit of righteousness that comes through Jesus Christ – to the glory and Praise of God." Philippians 1: 9-11 (NIV).

FINAL THOUGHTS

I hope you found something inspirational in my story. Unlike a fairy tale it does not have a happy ending; instead, it has a happy beginning! This is not the end. As my friend Colton Bradshaw says, this is just the beginning!

STEVEN STEHLE

STEVEN STEHLE

Steve is an ardent history buff who especially enjoys reading historical novels. He is a grateful, recovered addict that has been spreading the word of God's redemptive power to all who will listen. Once a broken man, he is now whole and enjoys the fellowship of other believers, exploring the thoughts and wisdom of others and seeking God's direction for his life. A passionate storyteller, in church or in public, he is often found surrounded by children that love him.

www.ingramcontent.com/pod-product-compliance
Lightning Source LLC
Chambersburg PA
CBHW072003110526
44592CB00012B/1189